Esse ce

Studies in Paul's Missionary Strategy

Essentials of Missionary Service

Studies in Paul's Missionary Strategy

Kenneth C. Fleming

OM
publishing

Copyright © 2000 Kenneth C. Fleming
First published in 2000 by OM Publishing

06 05 04 03 02 01 00   7 6 5 4 3 2 1

OM Publishing is an imprint of Paternoster Publishing,
PO Box 300, Carlisle, Cumbria, CA3 0QS, UK
and Paternoster Publishing USA
Box 1047, Waynesboro, GA 30830-2047

http:www.paternoster-publishing.com

The right of Kenneth C. Fleming to be identified as the Author
of this work has been asserted by him in accordance with the
Copyright, Design and Patent Act 1988.

British Library Cataloguing in Publication Data
A catalogue record for this book is available from the British
Library

ISBN 1-85078-354-3

Scripture taken from the
NEW AMERICAN STANDARD BIBLE ®,
copyright © 1960, 1962, 1963, 1968, 1971, 1972, 1973,
1975, 1977, 1995 by The Lockman Foundation.
Used by permission.

Cover Design by Mainstream, Lancaster
Typeset by WestKey Ltd, Falmouth, Cornwall
Printed in Great Britain by
Omnia Books Limited, Glasgow

Dedication

This book is dedicated to my son, James K. Fleming, whose ministry in Bogota, Colombia has been blessed by God.

Contents

Notes on the author

Kenneth C. Fleming

Ken Fleming was born in Seattle, Washington
and grew up in a strong Christian home. With
his brother Peter he was greatly influenced by
the Navigators during high school years. The
brothers both earned degrees at the University
of Washington in Seattle. They were both very
active in a thriving Brethren assembly nearby as
well as in the Inter Varsity Group on Campus.
Ken married Helena in 1950 and in 1951 they
were commended to the Lord's work by their
assembly for service in South Africa. A few
months later Peter left for Ecuador where he lost
his life with Jim Elliot seeking to reach the
people of the Auca tribe.

Ken and Helena studied Zulu and eventually
moved to the city of Durban. There 11 Zulu
speaking churches were planted over the next
20 years. Ken concentrated on an evening Bible

school for the preparation of leadership. After 25 years in Africa Ken accepted the position as head of the Missions Department at Emmaus Bible College, in the Chicago area. The college has since moved to Dubuque, Iowa. He has been teaching missions at Emmaus for the past 23 years. In addition he frequently speaks at conferences and ministers to missionaries in the field. Numerous articles have come from his pen as well as six books, all on biblical or missionary themes.

Foreword

Mission today is driven by strategies, plans, and targets for the evangelisation of the world. The last decades of the twentieth century have seen an ever-increasing focus on missions in many parts of the church of Jesus Christ, as the traditional sending countries of the west were joined in this enterprise by newly emerging sending countries. As the pages of this book inform us, more people have come to faith in Christ this century, than in any previous century in history and that number continues to grow. It is easy to assume that this is the result of our programmes rather than the sovereign work of the Holy Spirit, through the proclamation of the Word of God. Therefore the danger is that in the multiplication of programmes and setting of targets, the ultimate purpose of mission, that of presenting men and women mature in Christ, is forgotten. Thus it is important to examine our foundations and ensure that they are Biblical, so that what is built will last.

Ninety years ago, Roland Allen challenged the missionary world of his day in his classic text 'Missionary Methods: Saint Paul's or Ours?' He asked his generation to examine with more care how they went about the task of fulfilling Christ's commission and compare their methods with those of Paul the apostle. This was necessary in that era when Western methods and culture were unquestioned in their supremacy, and it is equally necessary in the global marketplace of missions today, where varying strategies and even theologies compete for our attention and support.

Ken Fleming sets out to achieve this same goal by examining the major biblical principles that controlled the missionary life of Paul, the greatest of all missionaries. Although the world has changed radically since Allen wrote in 1912, and even more so since the Roman world of the first century, the simple biblical principles followed by Paul are still relevant and applicable today in any context and culture. So an examination of the strategy of Paul the evangelist, Paul the teacher and Paul the church planter, should be a frequent exercise for all who are interested in evangelism and mission.

The author is well qualified for this task and writes from a lifetime of experience in mission. 25 years of service among the Zulu people of

South Africa provided a practical apprenticeship and exposure to the difficulties as well as
the successes of missionary service. The Pauline
principles he sets out in this book were applied
in a real life situation, and churches planted
then, continue to develop and grow under
indigenous leadership many years later. A
prolonged period spent teaching missions to
successive generations of students at Emmaus
Bible College has allowed him to mould his students in Paul's methods, while a wide exposure
to mission in many parts of the world has added
to his convictions that Paul's model is simple,
biblical and transferable to any cultural context.

The contents of this book were originally
given as three talks presented at Echoes Day in
Westminster Chapel London in October 1986.
These were produced in simple format by
Echoes of Service under the title 'Missionary
Service in the Life of Paul'. The original lectures
have been expanded and illustrated with contemporary examples of how these principles
have been successfully applied in different
fields. We believe that this book will be of value
to anyone who is involved in evangelism and
church planting, especially if this is being done
in a cross-cultural context. However it will also
be of interest to any follower of Jesus Christ who
wants to be more effective in life and witness
and wants to have a more biblical understanding of the priorities of mission. We are grateful

to Ken Fleming for making this available in an
enlarged format and hope and pray that it will
be used by God to further the supreme and all-
important task of making Jesus Christ known to
our world today.

Dr Ian Burness
Echoes of Service, Bath

Preface

Michael Borodin was sent to China in 1923 by Lenin as a special advisor from the Communist Party in Russia. His job was to help reorganize the Kuomintang into a highly disciplined central party. His most promising students were Sun Yat Sen, Chiang Kai-shek, and a young man from Vietnam named Ho Chi-minh.

Borodin was interviewed by an American correspondent concerning his purpose to 'take over China for a Communist movement.' The correspondent finally said, 'You are too few. You'll never do it.'

'Oh yes we will,' came the cool reply, 'You forget, young man, that I am not here for my health, comfort, or personal success. I am totally dedicated to the cause of the Communist movement.'

After a long silence, Borodin began to murmur, half to himself, 'You know,' he mused, 'I used to read the New Testament. It is the most wonderful story ever told. That man Paul, he was a real revolutionary. I take my hat off to him.'

Suddenly Borodin whirled around and shook his fist in the face of the correspondent. 'But where do you find him today?' he shouted. 'Answer me that. Where do you find him today?'

Borodin's question is an excellent starting point for an enquiry into the missionary work of the apostle Paul. Where do you find him today? Where do you find missionaries who are totally dedicated to practising the simple yet profound principles which Paul used in the early church? A re-examination of the Pauline strategy of missions may do much to sharpen our own focus and to make us more effective ambassadors for the Lord Jesus Christ.

There are more Christian missionaries in more places today than at any time in history. They have become increasingly involved in specialized ministries from 'a to z' (agriculture to zoology). Growing specialization holds a danger of which we ought to be aware. The danger is that in our emphasis on special ministries we may lose the primary principles of the Great Commission. The result is that a decreasing percentage of missionaries are directly involved in the basics of evangelism, teaching, and church planting. Instead the tools of mission, such as social improvement, have become ends in themselves.

Paul used tools, but concentrated on the primary principles. This study is concerned with the New Testament record of Paul's missionary strategy. It is a restatement of biblical missionary essentials which are seen in the life of the apostle.

1

What are the Essentials of Missions?

The twentieth century has been a missionary century. During the course of the last hundred years more people have come to faith in Christ than in any previous century in history. Of the approximately 6 billion people in the world 5.7% claim to be evangelical.[1] Evangelical Christianity is growing fast in both the number of its converts and the number of cultural areas it occupies. A significant part of this thrust has been and continues to be spearheaded by cross-cultural missions. In other words mission is booming! For most of us that is good news.

As we enter the third millennium since the Great Commission was given it may be good for today's disciples to re-examine the purpose

[1] Johnstone, Patrick, Operation World, OM Publishing, 1995.

and character of missions in the light of
Scripture. The biblical record gives us a great
deal of information about the growth and
development of Christianity in the first
century. It provides us not only with a
historical model of missions but with a practical handbook for carrying it out.

The purpose of this chapter is to carefully
examine the activities which are essential to
biblical missions. When we speak of essentials,
we mean those elements of missions which are
indispensable to the task. These indispensable
activities ought to characterize every
missionary effort. Modern missions are often
looked at as a collection of special tasks.
Linguists, publishers, evangelists, elementary
school teachers, Bible teachers, executives,
secretaries, pilots and mechanics, doctors and
dentists, counsellors, artists, church planters
and peanut planters – all are missionaries.
Many people make the mistake of seeing each
task in isolation as being vitally important,
particularly if they themselves are involved in
it. It will be helpful for you to consider missions,
not so much as one of a large number of tasks to
be performed in cross-cultural settings, but as a
mandate from the Lord Jesus Christ which
should be carried out by every worker, no
matter what else may occupy their time. The
mandate is given to us in Scripture and its
elements are few. Everyone who calls himself or

herself a missionary ought to be involved in these basic essential activities.

Missions in the Book of Acts

As we discuss the essentials of missions we also ought to be clear as to what we mean by the word 'missions'. The only worthwhile answer must come from the Word of God. We will find it clearly revealed in the divinely inspired documents about first century missions in the Book of Acts. It is in Acts that we learn of the formation, growth and outreach of the church. The church was formed at Pentecost when the Spirit of God empowered the Jewish Christian believers in Jerusalem for the new era which was starting (Acts 2). Following Pentecost God allowed two other cultural groups of believers to have a Pentecost-like experience – the Samaritans (Acts 8) and the Gentiles (Acts 10). By the similarity of their experience God was assuring them, and us, that the new entity He was forming from different peoples was one body.

The first ten chapters of Acts summarize God's formation of the church in three different cultural settings – Jewish (Acts 2–7), Samaritan (Acts 8), and Gentile (Acts 10–11). Up until this point in the record the church was centred in Jerusalem and strongly Jewish in character. The

Christian Jews brought animal sacrifices and offerings to the temple where the rituals of Judaism continued without interruption. They expected that Christianity would maintain its Jewish flavour, but God had larger plans for His church; He knew that neither the Samaritans nor the Gentiles could be incorporated into ritualistic Judaism. His plan was to build the church as a separate entity from Judaism. Jewish Christians would have to come out from Judaism and meet as one with all other believers without cultural distinction.

This beginning of the church with its new form is recorded for us by Luke in Acts 11. It happened in the city of Antioch in Syria. The Jewish believers there were joined by men from North Africa and Cyprus who began to evangelize Greeks as well as Jews without distinction. A large number believed and the first New Testament church was established from those converts. The church in Jerusalem sent Barnabas to assure themselves that God was in this significant change. Barnabas recognized the movement of God and encouraged the new work. Later Barnabas brought Saul from Tarsus to teach them (Acts 11:19–30).

The church grew quickly with appointed leaders who are next seen praying for God's guidance as to outreach. The Spirit of God made it very clear to the leaders that they were to release two of their number for evangelism in other places. These two were Barnabas and Saul (Acts 13:1–4). They were publicly commended (literally 'handed over') to God for the work of evangelism and church planting in which they were to engage (compare Acts 13:1–4 with 14:26).

Barnabas and Saul took with them a promising young man by the name of John Mark forming a threesome. They began what we call the first missionary journey by sailing from Antioch to the island of Cyprus and then on to Asia Minor. The record of this journey is found in chapters 13 and 14 of Acts and should be carefully studied by every student of missions. In these two chapters we find the basics of New Testament missionary life and practice. The elements of biblical missionary strategy are clearly revealed. The model of New Testament missions is displayed for us. Not only was it closely followed by all subsequent missions recorded in Acts, it remains the model for the church until the end of the age.

Mission Cyprus (Acts 13:4–12)

In this brief section we read that the small team first sailed to the nearest port on the eastern side of Cyprus. Several things should be noted here, Barnabas was a native of Cyprus so it was understandable that he had a burden to witness in his home territory. His Levitical ancestry and

Paul's rabbinical training in Jerusalem gave them special access to synagogues. Synagogues were important to their evangelistic strategy because they could find both Jews who were regular worshippers and interested Gentiles there. Many Gentiles in the first century had become disgusted with the pantheon of Greek and Roman gods and were attracted to the monotheism of the Jews. These Gentiles are referred to as 'God-fearers' or 'proselytes' (converts to Judaism) in the New Testament (Acts 10:2, 22, 13:16, 26, 43 etc.). Thus for Barnabas and Paul the synagogues contained the people most receptive to the gospel at that time. No wonder that they were a prime target in their evangelism.

On Cyprus they first taught the Word of God in synagogues of the eastern city, Salamis. Then they continued westward, presumably evangelizing as they went. When they came to the western city of Paphos the proconsul summoned them so he too could hear the Word of God. Opposition arose from a Jewish false prophet called Bar-Jesus who tried to turn the proconsul away from the faith. Paul confronted this man and pronounced temporary blindness on him. Bar-Jesus was led away blind, but the proconsul believed the message (vv. 5–12). To summarize this first 'campaign' they preached the gospel in the two major cities of Cyprus with the result that at least one person believed.

Mission Antioch (Acts 13:13–41)

From Paphos they sailed north to Perga on the south coast of what is now Turkey. John left them there while Paul and Barnabas continued overland to Pisidian Antioch. This was in an area of the Anatolian plateau known as South Galatia. Again they went to the synagogue and were again given opportunity to speak to the Jews and Gentiles there ('Men of Israel and you who fear God'). Paul stood up and gave a masterful gospel message based on the history of the Israelites. He touched on the history of King David from whom 'God has brought Israel a Saviour, Jesus'. He explained Jesus' ministry, His rejection, crucifixion, burial and resurrection. He proved the resurrection by quoting Ps. 16:10 and then preached the forgiveness of sins. The result was that many of both Jews and proselytes believed the words of Paul and Barnabas.

On the next Sabbath a great crowd gathered to listen. The Jews, however became envious and stirred up many in the city, so much so that Paul announced that he was 'turning to the Gentiles' because the Jews repudiated the truth of the gospel. This encouraged the Gentiles, many of whom believed. Jewish opposition grew so that Paul and Barnabas were driven out of the city (Acts 13:13–50). In summary, they preached to everyone who would listen which led to opposition from the Jews. A number of both Jews and Gentiles believed and became disciples 'filled with joy and the Holy Spirit' (Acts 13:52). That was the beginning of the church in Antioch.

Mission Iconium (Acts 13:51–14:7)

In Iconium, the next major city, a similar chain of events happened. With less detail in Scripture, we do know that they began in the synagogue and 'a great multitude believed, both of Jews and of Greeks'. Attesting miracles confirmed the message. Again opposition from the Jews caused even some Gentiles to be against the apostles. When mistreatment and stoning arose they fled from the city, but they left behind a group of believers. Note the pattern – preaching in the synagogue, some believed, then opposition from the Jews.

Mission Lystra (Acts 14: 8–20)

They fled south to a town called Lystra. In Lystra there was no synagogue because there were too few Jews, so they began to preach in the market place. There they met a lame man, who had never walked, listening to the word. As Paul preached he became aware of the lame man's faith, so he commanded him, 'Stand up on your feet'. The man leaped up and began to walk causing the pagan people to think that

Barnabas and Paul were gods. When the missionaries understood that they were about to make a pagan sacrifice to them they stopped them by shouting that they too were just men. They urged the people of Lystra to turn to the living God, the Creator.

While all these things were going on, opposing Jews who had followed the apostles from Antioch and Iconium were able to stir up the crowd to turn against Paul. They dragged him out of the city and stoned him leaving him for dead. As the new converts gathered around him, Paul revived. He stayed overnight with them and left the next day. Three of the new converts were Timothy, Eunice and Lois who are mentioned elsewhere in the New Testament. These three and other converts are called disciples – disciplined learners who are serious. In summary, they preached the gospel in Lystra and some, called disciples, believed. Opposition came as in the past from the Jews who stoned Paul leaving him for dead.

Mission Derbe (Acts 14:20–21)

The fourth and final city of South Galatia to which they went was Derbe. We read almost no details of the mission there except that they preached the gospel and made many disciples.

Note the pattern thus far in each of the four cities. First, preaching in the most opportune place, whether synagogue or market place. Second, response by those called disciples. The difference between a disciple and a mere believer is that a disciple continues to grow in his faith and become active. Third, the seriousness and activity of their faith provoked opposition from unbelievers.

Establishing Churches (Acts 14:21–23)

Paul's missionary activity on his first missionary journey comes to a climax. He and Barnabas had done their best to evangelize the people of four cities in South Galatia. Many in all four cities became believers by believing the good news. They also became disciples by studying the truth of Scripture. It is summarized for us in verses 21–22.

'And after they had preached the gospel to that city and had made many disciples, they returned to Lystra and to Iconium and to Antioch, strengthening the souls of the disciples, encouraging them to continue in the faith and saying "Through many tribulations we must enter the kingdom of God" '.

Note the two main thrusts of the apostles. First to evangelize and then to teach the new believers.

One thing remained in their task. It is stated in verse 23. 'And when they had appointed elders for them in every church, having prayed with fasting, they commended them to the Lord in whom they had believed'. Before Paul and Barnabas left the area, they established churches. They saw to it that each new church had leadership in the form of multiple elders who would be responsible for the care of the church and for its order. Only then was their task finished. Only then did they leave. The following verses go on to tell us that they went back to Syrian Antioch 'from which they had been commended to the grace of God for the work *that they had accomplished*' (Italics mine, v. 26).

What are Missions?

We must carefully observe that Paul's missionary work was 'accomplished' which means they had fulfilled their mission. There are no missing elements. They had finished the task for which they had been commended by the believers in Syrian Antioch. What was their mission? Plainly the answer is that it was to establish churches like the one from which they had come in Syrian Antioch. What were its essentials? There are three. First, to evangelize the unsaved. Second, to teach the new believers so that they would become strong in the faith. Third, it was to establish structured churches. Evangelism, discipleship, church planting – these are the essentials and together they are missions. It means that if you are a biblical missionary, this is what you do.

Contemporary Models

There are many examples of biblical work going on in our world. We are going to use four of these works as models in the course of this study. All four are in cross-cultural settings speaking four languages and located on three continents. They are practising the biblical strategy of missions and have all been blessed by God. One is in the Flemish speaking part of Belgium. The second is in the Zulu area of South Africa. The third is in Bogota, the capital city of Colombia. And the fourth is in eastern Austria. Each was a pioneer work, not building on previously established foundations. The missionaries are all from English speaking backgrounds and began by learning the language. They saw people saved by faith in Christ. They taught the believers the truth of Scripture and its application to their lives. Finally they established churches that were indigenous in the local cultural setting and no longer depended on the missionaries for help, either financial or pastoral. In each of the following chapters these churches will be used for illustrative purposes.

Other Forms of Missions?

Immediately questions will arise because we are accustomed to thinking of missions in much broader terms than the above. We think of institutional social programmes such as schools, hospitals, clinics, orphanages, agricultural help etc. We think of missionary assistance programmes in specialties such as aviation, translation, literature, audio-visual techniques, technological innovations etc. We think too of crisis programmes for the human condition such as disaster relief, refugee work, urban redevelopment, pregnancy centres, child abuse programmes, literacy programmes etc. All of these efforts stem from real problems and are meeting real needs. They are staffed by thousands of God's people many of whom are termed 'missionaries'.

As we look at these programmes in the light of biblical missions all of them are worth while. All of them express in one way or another the Christian response to a needy world, either to show the compassion of Christ or to assist the missionary to be more efficient in his presentation of the gospel. Missionaries from the time of the Moravians in the 1700s have sought to meet the needs of the human condition from two different perspectives. One was to express the love of God by acts of compassion. This is the same for all people everywhere.

The other way in which these activities were used was as the 'handmaid to the gospel'. For example; early missionaries in Africa learned and used the rudiments of medicine, education, dentistry, literacy, child care etc. as an aid to what they saw as their primary task which was to preach the gospel, disciple believers and establish churches. With medicine, which was not otherwise available, they won a hearing for their message. It was the same with orphanages and literacy classes; with education they were able to provide a wanted skill in a changing world. At the same time they were preparing the young church to read the Scriptures for themselves. With translation, they prepared the Scriptures in the language of the people. The list could be extended.

As the 'handmaid of the gospel' this kind of social activity assisted the missionaries in their primary task. The early missionaries seldom lost their focus amidst all of these activities. They used them as tools to promote their clearly established goal which was a strong indigenous church in every area. They were careful never to wander from the centrality of the gospel. However as time went on and the social activities became institutionalized, more and more specialists came who had special skills in their respective fields of expertise, and often, less vision for the larger purpose and the essentials of mission. The trend has continued to this day when more and more specialists are being recruited to meet the ever growing demands of cross-cultural work.

Without getting into debate over the relative value of any or all of these specialties, we are only concerned here with their relationship to the essentials of missions. I think it can be established with no difficulty that biblically speaking the essentials of missions are those outlined above and that other programmes, while valuable, are not essential to missions. Paul travelled on his second missionary journey with a physician, Luke, but nowhere do we read of any medical practice as being part of his mission. He lived in a world where up to 80% of the people were slaves, but we read nothing of any programmes to free them. He did send one slave, Onesimus, back to his master, Philemon. Ninety percent of the people could not read, but there were no literacy programmes mentioned.

This is not intended to be an argument that the silence in Scripture on any particular topic means that Scripture disallows or forbids such practice. Scripture is very much on the side of all acts of human compassion for the Lord's sake. All believers should be marked by compassion, whether in or out of missions. Indeed acts of human compassion have always been and will be used in conjunction with the message of the gospel.

The plea of this chapter is that anyone who is involved in Christian missions ought to be involved in the basics of evangelism, discipleship and church planting. It is wonderful that other skills in fields such as medicine, education or aviation can be used for God, but they should not be confused with the essentials of missions. A missionary doctor ought to bear in mind that he/she is first a missionary and second a doctor. If a local assembly commends a couple to work cross-culturally as missionaries they should assure themselves that the couple are competent in the basics, no matter what other skills they may be able to use for God. It is great to have the linguistic skills to translate Scripture, but don't forget to lead people to Christ, disciple them in the faith and get them involved in the local church. It is great to be an agronomist with ideas for better farming, but the primary task is the essential task. Your suitability ought to be judged on whether you can lead a soul to Christ and train him/her as a disciple much more than on your qualifications as an agronomist. In all these extra skills this is what is important.

Conclusion

In conclusion let us remember that the scope of missions is large and may include any of a large number of skills, abilities and compassionate acts. However the essentials of missions as given in holy Scripture are basic to the mandate given to us by the Lord Jesus and to the model left to us by Paul and his companions. Stick to the basics. The following chapters emphasize the three major biblical principles of missions as they have been modelled for us in the missionary life of Paul and his companions.

2

Evangelism in the Ministry of Paul

There are more Christian missionaries in more places today than at any time in history. They have become increasingly involved in specialized ministries from 'a to z' (agriculture to zoology). Growing specialization holds a danger of which we ought to be aware. The danger is that in our emphasis on special ministries we may lose the primary principles of the Great Commission. The result is that a decreasing percentage of missionaries are directly involved in the basics of evangelism, teaching, and church planting. Instead the tools of missions, such as school and hospital are becoming the goals of mission. Paul used tools, but concentrated on the primary principles. This study is concerned with the New Testament record of Paul's missionary strategy. It is a restatement of biblical missionary principles which are seen in the life of the apostle.

Without doubt Paul is the most outstanding Christian in the New Testament. His razor-sharp mind formulated the great doctrines of salvation. His remarkable vision enabled him to evangelize a significant part of the Greek world in the first century. His enormous capacity for caring love has rarely been equalled. Paul stands alone as the great exponent of New Testament Christianity. Not only did he live it himself, he communicated it to others. This communication of Christ to others is evangelism.

The effectiveness of Paul's evangelistic outreach is unquestioned. Where he went people were saved. He sought out his own people and shared the gospel with them. Some responded. He evangelized Gentiles with equal fervour and large numbers were converted. As a result local churches were planted along the whole coastline of the Aegean Sea. The zeal of new believers carried the gospel rapidly inland resulting in many more congregations of new believers. The expansion was so effective that Paul and his fellow evangelists were accused of 'turning the world upside down.' Paul has left us a model of evangelism which we do well to study. Our own effectiveness can be increased if we understand and apply the Pauline model. Many of us have failed to do this.

Our failure can be attributed to several factors. First, perhaps, is the supposition that in nineteen hundred years the world has changed so much first century models are no longer applicable. The changes are real and dramatic most certainly. But the models remain unaffected because they are concerned with principle rather than form. Time does not change them.

A second reason for failure to follow Paul's model of evangelism is our tendency to rely on technology. In comparison Paul seems so limited. He could only travel 20 miles in a day. He could only preach to those within earshot. His literature was limited to one handwritten copy at a time. He had no financial resource from his sending church and no more organization than a small team-on-the-move could supply. Our reliance on technology may easily blind us to the biblical principles which could teach us to use that technology effectively.

A third factor in our failure to follow Paul comes from our own traditions. We tend to base our evangelism on our own narrow cultural heritage rather than on broad biblical principles. The methodology of our heritage may or may not be effective from one generation to another. The principles are more basic and allow a variety of methods to be used in their application.

'Methods are many,
 Principles are few
Methods may change,
 Principles never do.'

In our study of Pauline evangelism we will be focusing on the principles underlying his methods. This will allow us to use Paul's principles although our methodology may be different. For example, the method of preaching the gospel in synagogues is based on the principle of going to the place where there are the most potential converts. In Paul's day that place was the synagogue but it would not be so in our country today.

Finally, we may fail to follow Paul's model because we assume that the world conditions in his day made it uniquely 'ripe' for evangelism. So much so, that it would be useless for us to follow his model. It is true that in the providence of God there was a combination of factors which did influence the spread of the gospel. However, this does not alter the principle that 'now is the day of salvation' (2 Cor. 6:2), and God is at work to accomplish it.

Any consideration of Paul the evangelist will examine the man himself in his role as evangelist. It will look at the message he preached and the people (world) he reached. Finally, it will look at the strategy he used as he made choices regarding his evangelistic ministry.

Paul's Role as an Evangelist

As a 'man for all seasons' Paul excelled in many roles: theologian, teacher, strategist, etc. But in none did he succeed more than in his role as an evangelist. His whole post-conversion life was marked by a burning desire to communicate Christ to people. As soon as he was converted to the Lord Jesus Christ and was baptized, 'immediately he began to proclaim Jesus in synagogues saying, "He is the Son of God" ' (Acts 9:20). As long as he lived, his passionate zeal for evangelism continued. In the final chapter of his last letter he was still pleading with Timothy, 'Do the work of an evangelist' (2 Tim. 4:5).

The Motivating Influences

Paul's evangelistic zeal was influenced by several factors.

His conversion

The first of these was his own conversion. As Saul, the Pharisee, he had been a zealot for the anti-Jesus movement. By persecuting the disciples he thought he was doing God a favour. The Damascus journey was part of his anti-Jesus campaign, when suddenly he was confronted with the light, the voice, and the vision of the risen Christ. There was no mistaking the message from heaven. 'I am Jesus' (Acts 9:5). At that instant the proud Saul became the penitent sinner at the feet of the Lord Jesus Christ. He never forgot that moment. The many references to his conversion in his own writings and three lengthy accounts of it in Acts testify to the fact that Paul was strongly affected by this incident in his life (Acts 9:22, 26).

Paul's conversion dramatically changed his life, and he came to expect the same kind of change in others. Conversion to him was not mere intellectual assent to a set of facts. Nor was it merely an emotional experience resulting from certain stimuli. It was an encounter with Christ in which the sinner acknowledged both his own lostness and also the saving work of the risen and glorified Lord Jesus Christ. Having met Jesus Christ himself, Paul considered that his work as an evangelist was to lead others to the same encounter.

His calling

Paul's role as an evangelist was also influenced by his calling. The second question he asked while kneeling in the dust of the Damascus road was, 'What shall I do, Lord?' (Acts 22:10). The answer was clear, and it was confirmed by godly Ananias that Paul had been chosen by the Lord to be a witness to all men of what he had seen and heard. He was to bear the name of the Lord Jesus before Gentiles and kings and the sons of Israel (Acts 9:15; 22:15; 26:16–17). He was called to be an apostle (a sent one) of Jesus Christ (1 Cor. 1:1; Rom. 1:1; 2 Tim. 1:1, etc.). God called him to witness in a special way to Gentiles. Thus, he refers to himself as 'an

apostle of Gentiles' (Rom. 11:13). His calling to
evangelism was unmistakable. Paul never
forgot it. It had come from the Lord in glory.

The lostness of those outside Christ
His role as an evangelist was also influenced by
the lostness of people outside Christ. He viewed
men as being under the wrath of God because of
their unrighteousness (Rom. 1:18). He knew
they all had sinned and were accountable to a
holy God who must judge them. He saw them
as 'having no hope and without God in the
world' (Eph. 2:12). He knew there was a day
coming when the Lord would be revealed 'in
flaming fire dealing out retribution to those
who do not know God and to those who do not
obey the gospel of our Lord Jesus. And these
will pay the penalty of eternal destruction away
from the presence of the Lord' (2 Thess. 1:7–9).
The lost condition of the Jews caused Paul
intense grief. 'I have great sorrow and unceas-
ing grief in my heart' (Rom. 9:2).

The love of Christ
Another influence on Paul as an evangelist was
the love of Christ revealed on the cross.
Although Paul had not been there at the
crucifixion, it influenced his life and witness in a
remarkable way. The cross was central to his
preaching. 'I determined to know nothing
among you except Jesus Christ and Him

crucified' (1 Cor. 2:2). The cross was his boast
(Gal. 6:14). It was a symbol of the love of the Lord
Jesus Christ. That love, he said, was the control-
ling force in his life. It urged him to a ministry of
reconciliation as an ambassador of Christ (2 Cor.
5:14–20). Isaac Watts, the hymnwriter, captures
it very well.

'When I survey the wondrous cross
  On which the Prince of glory died,
My richest gain I count but loss
  And pour contempt on all my pride.

Were the whole realm of nature mine,
  That were an offering far too small
Love so amazing, so divine,
  Demands my heart, my life, my all.'

His debt to the unsaved
Finally, Paul's role as an evangelist was
influenced by his perception of debt to the
unsaved. He calls himself a debtor 'under obligation both to the Greeks and to barbarians'
(Rom. 1:14). As an heir of the kingdom, he was
spiritually wealthy. In relation to the lost
around him, he felt the obligation to share the
good news. It was a debt of love to them. He
wrote to the Corinthians, 'For if I preach the
gospel I have nothing to boast of, for I am under
compulsion; for woe is me if I do not preach the
gospel' (1 Cor. 9:16).

Thus Paul's role as an evangelist was influenced by his own conversion, by his calling from God, by the lostness of mankind, by the love of Christ displayed on the cross, and by his own obligation to the unsaved.

The Goals of Paul's Evangelism

These influences motivated Paul to evangelism, but what were his goals? What did he expect to accomplish? Several passages make his evangelistic goals distinct. Upon his return from the first missionary journey with Barnabas, 'they began to report all things that God had done with them and how he had opened a door of faith to the Gentiles' (Acts 14:27). To the Romans he spoke 'of the grace that was given me from God to be a minister of Christ Jesus to the Gentiles, ministering as a priest the gospel of God' (Rom. 15:15–16). His goals included also a response from his hearers. The letter to the Romans continues with 'what Christ has accomplished through me, resulting in the obedience of the Gentiles by word and deed . . . so that from Jerusalem and round about as far as Illyricum I have fully preached the gospel of Christ. And thus I aspired to preach the gospel, not where Christ was already named' (Rom. 15:18–20).

Thus Paul's evangelistic goals included the preaching of the gospel to Gentiles, especially in unevangelized areas. He earnestly sought the response of faith in Christ from his hearers. When this happened, he could say, 'I have fully preached the gospel.' A selection of quotes from Paul's later letters confirms this goal:

> To me . . . this grace was given, to preach to the Gentiles the unfathomable riches of Christ (Eph. 3:8).
> Pray . . . that utterance may be given to me . . . to make known with boldness the mystery of the gospel for which I am an ambassador in chains (Eph. 6:19–20).
> I was made a minister . . . that I might fully carry out the preaching of the word of God . . ., to make known what is the riches of the glory of this mystery among the Gentiles (Col. 1:25–27).
> The Lord stood with me and strengthened me in order that through me the proclamation might be fully accomplished and that all the Gentiles might hear (2 Tim. 4:17).

The last quote, written very shortly before Paul's death, still reflects the distinct purpose of his ministry of evangelism to Gentiles. He had not wavered during the entire length of his life of service.

Paul's Message as an Evangelist

Central to Paul's role as an evangelist and his goal of evangelism was his message – the

evangel. It is important for us to examine the
content of the message and then its application
to differing groups of people. The underlying
truths of Paul's evangel were consistently the
same, though their application to peoples in
diverse cultural settings varied considerably.
Missionaries today should always be careful to
make this distinction.

The Content of his Message

Three unalterable and universal truths under-
lie Paul's evangelistic preaching: First, man's
sinful condition and God's consequent judgement. Second, God's gracious provision of
salvation through Christ's finished work.
Third, man's present opportunity to repent
and believe in the Lord Jesus Christ for
salvation.

At Paul's own conversion these basic truths
were made known to him. He was made aware
that he was a sinner working in opposition to
God, 'kicking against the goads' (Acts 26:14).
He then saw Christ raised from the grave and
fully understood that this was proof of a
completed work of atonement. Finally, he
verbally acknowledged Christ, the Lord and
turned to become a bondservant of His from
that point on. The frequent occasions when Paul
made reference to his conversion indicate the
importance that it had.

The same three truths mark Paul's preaching to his own people, the Jews. The sermon in the synagogue of Pisidian Antioch is a model of missionary approach to Jews (Acts 13:14–41). In it Paul uses their history of failure to show that God was leading toward the coming of a Saviour. He also showed that the prophecies of the Saviour in the Old Testament were fulfilled in the life, death, and resurrection of Jesus, the Messiah. Finally, he offered them forgiveness of sin through believing Him (Acts 13:38–39). This forgiveness and the freedom it brings were never available through Moses and the law.

In the context of preaching to Gentile audiences, Paul still emphasized the three basic truths. When he spoke to the Greek philosophers in Athens, the truths were there, even if given in an abbreviated form (Acts 17:19–31). He told them God would judge the world, implying that the world needed judging because of sin. He told them of the Lord Jesus as the Man appointed by God and raised from the dead, implying that God was satisfied with a finished work. He also urged them to repent from idolatry, the result of which was that some men and women 'believed' (v. 34).

Cultural Sensitivity of his Presentation

The point is that Paul's basic message was always the same. The same great truths of the

gospel were consistently found in his own
conversion experience and in his evangelism
among both Jews and Gentiles. The importance
of this cannot be over-emphasized. We must
never compromise the basics. Paul's method of
approach, however, varied considerably. He
was sensitive to the culture of his hearers. While
his basic message was unchanging, his methods
of approach were flexible. His cultural sensitivity is clearly seen in the different presentations
of the same truths.

The Approach to Jews and God-fearers
In Pisidian Antioch Paul's audience was made
up of Jews and God-fearers (Gentiles who
attended Jewish synagogues and were interested in God and the Scripture). Here Paul
preached a significant evangelistic message
(Acts 13:15–41). To these people who already
believed in the inspiration of Scripture and the
coming of Messiah Paul began with a summary
of Israel's history from the time of their deliver-
ance from Egypt until King David (13:16–22).
All of this was well known. Then he reminded
them that according to the promise of the Scripture, a Saviour was to come from the line of
David (v. 23). This Saviour had been announced
by John but was rejected by Jewish leaders who
did not recognize Him nor the Old Testament
prophecies about Him. They themselves
fulfilled additional prophecies by condemning

Him and having Him put to death. This explanation answered the questions every Jew would ask regarding Jesus in relation to the Scriptures and in relation to the leaders who had rejected Him.

The clinching argument to these Jews was that God raised Jesus from the dead (v. 30) as the Scriptures had foretold. Paul quotes three Old Testament Scriptures in verses 33, 34 and 35 to prove that the resurrection was foretold (Ps. 2:7, Isa. 55:3, Ps. 16:10). This was followed by an invitation to believe in Jesus as Saviour and to receive forgiveness of sin. He closed with a quote from Habakkuk about God doing some things which were hard to believe (v. 41). There was an immediate response. The people wanted to hear more.

Paul's sensitivity to their background and culture is obvious. They knew their own history and believed the Scriptures. Paul uses these to show that out of their history and Scriptures the promised Saviour would come. He then steps from the known to the unknown by showing that the man Jesus was the promised Saviour. Neither Jesus' rejection nor His death should be a stumbling block to their faith for both are described in Scripture. Therefore, they could have forgiveness of sin which was not available through the Law of Moses. Salvation was explained to them in terms to which they could easily relate.

The approach to Greek idol worshippers
The next time Paul preached the good news the
circumstances were different. Although he did
not have the opportunity to finish his message,
what we do know is instructive. Paul and
Barnabas arrived in Lystra. Paul healed a lame
man, and a crowd soon gathered. The idol-
worshipping crowd of local people jumped to
the conclusion that Paul and Barnabas were
Greek gods. Paul took the opportunity to preach
the gospel until he was stopped. In a different
cultural context he used another approach from
that at Pisidian Antioch. Jewish history and
Scriptures were not his starting point (Acts
14:8–18).

Instead he used the immediate context of
Greek gods. He identified himself and Barnabas
as being ordinary people with the same nature
as the people of Lystra. He stated that the mortal
gods of the Greeks were vain, but he and
Barnabas had come to bring good news so they
could turn to the living God who was immortal.
The true God is the Creator of all things. He is
the God of history who permits the ebb and
flow of nations, and He is the God of providence
who provides man with food and happiness as
a witness to His nature. Paul was unable to
continue speaking on this occasion, but enough
is recorded to underline his wisdom in using
culturally relevant terms.

The approach to Greek philosophers

A third example of Paul's cultural sensitivity in evangelism is given in his message to the philosophers in Athens (Acts 17:16–32). Again both the occasion and the cultural setting are used to advantage by Paul, the effective communicator. His audience was made up of intellectual Athenians whose chief pursuit was in discussing new angles of philosophy. They had heard Paul preaching in the great market place of Athens and invited him to address them at Mars Hill. Paul took the opportunity gladly to address what might be called the 'Athens Philosophical Society.'

He had noticed an altar to an unknown god and used this observation to speak to them of the true God. He spoke of God as the creator of the world and the Lord of heaven and earth. He explained that God transcended material temples and did not need people to supply Him with anything. He Himself is the source of all life and of the commonality of mankind on earth. God appointed the lines and boundaries of nations making it possible for them to seek Him, because God is near to all of us.

Paul then quotes from a Greek poet, Aratus, who wrote that we are God's offspring. Therefore, we are not to reduce God to an artistic image of stone. God will judge the world through the appointed Man and therefore is now giving people the opportunity to

repent and turn to Him who is raised from the
dead

Paul's message in Athens was adapted to his
audience. They did not know the Scriptures, but
they did know the Greek poets. Paul begins
where they are and then moves forward to present the good news of Jesus Christ as Saviour and
Lord.

The approach to Roman governors
One further example of Paul's evangelism in a
cultural context is his message to the governors
Festus and Agrippa (Acts 26:1–32). They were
Roman political leaders, well educated, and also
familiar with Jewish Scriptures and aspirations.
To them Paul made a legal defense, but more
importantly, he made an evangelistic appeal. He
based his appeal on the personal testimony of his
own encounter with God. He linked his testimony to the Scriptures which were known to
Agrippa. He argued that his vision and call came
from God and that his message of forgiveness
was consistent with the Prophets and Moses.
They had predicted the suffering and the resurrection of Messiah. Festus interrupted, but Paul
turned to Agrippa with an appeal to believe in
Christ, the promised One. All this took place in
the context of a king's court, and Paul was able to
express himself in relevant terms.

So to four widely differing audiences Paul used
differing yet culturally sensitive approaches. To

the worshipping Jews and God-fearers in
Antioch, salvation comes through the Son of
David who is risen from the dead. To the
heathen Gentiles in Lystra he said that the
Creator God has left man a witness of His care.[1]
To the intellectuals in Athens he said that the one
true God was to judge the world. To the educated governors Paul gave personal testimony
and a Scripture-based appeal. In all these examples we see that Paul used approaches consistent
with the 'target' audience. His terminology and
argument were adapted in each circumstance to
the cultural background of his hearers.

Paul's Strategy as an Evangelist

Another important aspect of Paul's evangelistic
activity is the strategy he used. Strategy is the
plan of operations put into effect to accomplish
the goals. Paul was a disciplined strategist. He
did not run aimlessly (1 Cor. 9:26). He described
his evangelism as an orderly activity, 'so that
from Jerusalem and round about as far as
Illyricum I have fully preached the gospel of
Christ' (Rom. 15:19). This passage indicates a
progressive westward advance around the
coastline of the Mediterranean from present day

---

[1] Since Paul was interrupted, it cannot be assumed
that this would have been the full extent of his
message.

Palestine to the former Yugoslavia. Even as he wrote this letter to the Romans, he was planning to go farther westward to Spain (Rom. 15:24).

In his strategy Paul was striving for two general objectives. First, he sought the individual salvation of as many as possible. He evangelized his own people, the Jews. Systematically he went from synagogue to synagogue preaching the good news and actively seeking converts. He was consistently put out of these, and then he preached to Gentiles among whom far more converts were obtained. God was taking from them a people for His name (Acts 15:14). A second general objective was the establishment of churches (assemblies of the converts). Paul's evangelism aimed at church planting. Thus his strategy aimed at fulfilling these two general objectives. Let us note some important elements in Paul's evangelistic strategy.

Sovereign Operation of the Holy Spirit

First, there is the sovereign operation of the Holy Spirit. Before the human aspects enter in, there must be the realization that the Holy Spirit of God is at work. At the outset of the first missionary journey, it was the Spirit of God who made known to the leaders of the local church in Syrian Antioch that they were to set apart Barnabas and Saul 'for the work to which I have called them' (Acts 13:2). They were 'sent out by the Holy Spirit,' indicating that it was as much a divine activity as an ecclesiastical one. As they journeyed they were guided by the Spirit (Acts 16:6–7).

Dependence on God through Prayer

A second element in Paul's strategy is his dependence on God through prayer. The mission of evangelism was born in prayer, and the first two evangelists were sent out with the united prayers of the church of Antioch (Acts 13:2–3). Paul's gospel thrust was bathed in prayer. From prison he asked the Ephesians to pray that his gospel preaching might be effective. Pray 'that utterance may be given to me in the opening of my mouth to make known with boldness the mystery of the gospel for which I am an ambassador in chains; that in proclaiming it I may speak boldly as I ought to speak' (Eph. 6:19–20; cf. Col. 4:2–4). He asked the Thessalonians to pray for his group that the word of the Lord might spread rapidly (2 Thess. 3:1). Prayer was and is the lifeline of evangelism.

Church-based and Church-Orientated

Thirdly, Pauline evangelistic strategy is church-based and church-orientated. By this I mean that his evangelistic work started from a local church and resulted in the planting of new local churches. It began from the local church in Syrian Antioch. Barnabas and Saul were sent out with the implied understanding that their job was to carry the work of evangelism to the point where other churches like the one in Antioch would be established. After establishing four such churches: Lystra, Iconium, Antioch, and Derbe, they returned to Syrian Antioch and reported that they had accomplished the work for which they had been commended (Acts 14:16). No other agency was involved; they were commended by the local church alone. But the evangelism was only complete when a new church was formed.

> The mission of the church is missions.
> The mission of missions is the church.

Plurality of Workers

The fourth element in his strategy was the plurality of workers. Paul was not a 'lone wolf.' Like his Lord, he shared his ministry with other workers as intimate friends and co-labourers. The disciples of the Lord Jesus were constantly with Him, serving with Him and learning from Him. Paul, too, surrounded himself with others and gladly acknowledged their part in relation to him. He calls them 'fellow labourers,' 'fellow workers,' 'fellow soldiers,' 'fellow helpers,' 'fellow bond-servants,' and 'fellow prisoners' (Phil. 4:3; Rom. 16:3; Phil. 2:25; 2 Cor. 8:23; Col. 1:7; Rom. 16:7). He viewed them as his partners (2 Cor. 8:23).

No doubt Paul was conscious of his apostolic mission and responsibility as leader, but his letters reveal a wonderful relationship between himself and the co-workers. He speaks of them in the warmest of terms without any word of criticism except the lament that Demas had forsaken him (2 Tim. 4:10). They included both men and women, whose names Paul delights to leave on record: Timothy, Luke, Epaphras, Tychicus, Silvanus, Priscilla and Aquila, Phoebe, Epaphroditus, and Mary. The list could be enlarged.

Paul's excellence in organizing people was an important factor in his strategy. This is a point sometimes overlooked; yet it is a key to his effectiveness. He also identified himself with others on an equal basis. All but two of the letters written to New Testament churches are co-authored with one or more of his co-workers.[2]

Selection of Geographic Areas

Paul's strategy was also marked by a fifth element, his choice of areas of outreach. While

---

[2] Note the salutations in 1 and 2 Corinthians, Galatians, Philippians, Colossians, and 1 and 2 Thessalonians.

there does not appear to be any specific pre-determined plan, there does seem to be a general strategy for geographic movement. He certainly did not rely on mystical experiences for direction, although once he was directed by a vision (Acts 16:9). Paul thought first in terms of provincial areas. He went to Cyprus, Pamphylia, and Pisidia (South Galatia) on his first journey. On his second he again passed through Galatia and then tried to go to Asia and then Bithynia. However, the Holy Spirit did not allow him. Then he was called to Macedonia and later to Achaia. All these were provinces.

Within the provinces Paul selected population centres where Greek civilization as well as Roman administration and commerce flourished, usually with a strong Jewish influence. Cities such as Iconium, Troas, Philippi, Thessalonica, Athens, Corinth, and Ephesus were centres in the four provinces where Paul concentrated his mission. Paul was an urban strategist. Only once is it mentioned that he preached in the countryside surrounding the cities (Acts 14:6–7). Then within the cities Paul looked for gathering places of potential converts. The place where the greatest concentration of these might be found was usually the synagogue. This, then, was where he went. If there was no synagogue, he sought other places where potential converts gathered such as the 'agora' (market place).

Selection of Target Peoples

Sixthly, Paul's strategy included the selection of target peoples, those who appeared to be the most responsive to the gospel. He found these initially from two sources. He used contacts previously made through a web of relationships. His years in Syrian Antioch no doubt helped initially because of travelling commercial people who came from many places. Contacts multiplied as he and his team progressed from place to place. He also used his entree into synagogues where there were some Jews who were ready to believe in Jesus, their Messiah and also many God-fearing Gentiles. These Gentile God-fearers were particularly responsive to the gospel, and a great many of the early converts came from this group. Other interested people were found through the public preaching of the evangel in markets.

Resources, Financial and Personal

The final element in the evangelistic strategy of Paul is concerned with the material resources he obtained and used. There is no hint that his commending church in Antioch supported the outreach with financial help. We do know that Paul worked at tent making in Corinth (Acts 18:3). We also know that the mission churches already planted sent him funds (Phil. 4:16). Paul taught his converts to give through the local church (2 Cor. 8:1–9:15). It would appear, therefore, that the resources Paul and his fellow-workers used came from individuals and churches to whom they had preached and from their own labour. These resources were used principally in the personal and travel expenses of the workers and in assisting the needy believers such as the poor saints in Jerusalem (1 Cor. 16:1–3). Church buildings were not contemplated in New Testament mission strategy.

Contemporary Examples

These principles can be clearly seen in the work of Richard and Marina Haverkamp in Belgium. In 1970 they were sent out to that work by a local church in Wallenstein, Ontario, Canada. They moved to the Antwerp area with another Canadian couple and began to invite interested people to study the Bible with them. As a result several were saved and by April, 1972 there a number met regularly in their home as a local church. Haverkamp wrote, 'We knew why we were in Belgium; we knew that God had sent us there. We knew what our mission was – planting churches all over Flemish Belgium as quickly as possible. This we set out to do with youthful enthusiasm and with faith in

God.'[3] The Bible studies grew and within a year, almost 70 crowded into that room on Sundays. The believers rented an old store in a nearby suburb. With a growing number of disciples and newly appointed elders in place the Haverkamps moved to a new town to do it again. That is evangelism, and it continued moving from one town to another. Soon Belgian workers too were leading evangelistic Bible studies where people were saved and new churches were started all over Flemish speaking Belgium. By 1995 there were 28 churches with over 1500 believers.

Another example comes from Durban, South Africa where the author was a missionary. His work with Zulu people began on an established mission station in the country. Soon however, he realized the importance of the city of Durban to the future of the Zulu church. Together with two Zulu brothers he began evangelizing in the city. The method was different in a different cultural setting. Durban was a growing port city with multiplying job opportunities. Ever growing numbers of Zulus came from traditional life in the country to live and work in the city. Their life circumstances were in a state of change making them more open to receive the gospel. Because the Zulus in Durban had only recently arrived,

---

[3] Richard Haverkamp, 'God is at Work in Belgium,' *Missions* (June, 1988) p. 3

the missionaries evangelized using a traditional method as used in the country. The method involved leading a group of believers from house to house singing as they went and stopping in the houses of friends to give testimony and preach the gospel. This familiar method was accepted easily. Where there was interest, they would stay for hours and usually some would trust the Lord. As more were saved, other groups evangelized in the same way with a growing number of believers. Within 20 years there were a dozen Zulu assemblies formed in the area around the city of Durban.

Brian and Sheran Killins went to Bogota, Colombia in 1977. By 1979 a few new believers began to meet as a biblical church in their apartment. The new believers witnessed to friends and soon they leased a house for use as a church building and gospel centre. The lively music of the believers began to attract others in to listen to the music and to the gospel. When the believers saw how people were being attracted to the gospel meetings through music, they concentrated on improving its quality. The result was that larger numbers came, and larger numbers were saved. Those saved were then carefully discipled and churches with elders were formed. Now there are twelve thriving assemblies in Bogota. Every three months they have a combined meeting in a large rented hall with between 800 and 1200 people coming.

Almost always at these large gatherings they see others trust the Lord.

Our final example comes from lower Austria beginning in the city of St. Polten. In Austria the number of church spires might lead you to the conclusion that there are many true believers. This is not the case, though most Austrians would consider themselves to be Christians. The deadness of the old church has left the country with only the tiniest minority of true believers. The overwhelming majority of Austrians know nothing about the Bible and have rejected it as irrelevant.

Therefore those who came as missionaries to the country were also rejected. Floyd and Christine Schneider moved to Austria from Portland, Oregon in the early 1980s. They began to overcome these obstacles not by belonging to any mission agency or church but by making friends with Austrians. Through non-religious connections with students, writers and teachers, they slowly won their confidence and friendship. Only then did they ask them to study the Gospel of John in small groups. Some responded and by the time they had reached the middle chapters of John they had either been saved or left the study. Those who were saved have formed churches, sometimes amid strong opposition from family or community, but the work has grown. Floyd and Christine won a hearing and then they won souls.

Note that wise workers have evangelized in widely different areas – Belgium, South Africa, Colombia and Austria. The cultural settings were very different. The approaches to evangelism were very different, but each approach was relevant in its setting. The priority of evangelism in all four places was the same and God graciously blessed His Word to the saving of souls.

Conclusion

In conclusion, the implications of Pauline evangelism for us are clear. It may well be that we should rearrange our priorities to give evangelism much more emphasis. Institutional work and the pressure to get involved in social programmes have the tendency to seem urgent and to claim priority. The missionary with Paul's heart, however, will exclaim, 'Woe is me if I do not preach the gospel' (1 Cor. 9:16). We should also increase our versatility in being all things to all men. Not only should we be versatile ourselves, but we need to be more sensitive to the cultural context of those to whom we are ministering.

Our message must be kept as clear as was Paul's when he said, 'We preach Christ crucified' (1 Cor. 1:23). Finally, we must keep the spiritual side of our evangelism to the forefront. Unless the Lord builds the house they labour in vain who build it. The ministry of the Spirit of God and the prayers of the people of God are essential to the extension of the kingdom of God.

3

Teaching in the Ministry of Paul

Paul as a missionary was a great teacher as well as a great evangelist. Like his Master he was a maker of disciples, a trainer of men. His remarkable missionary success had as much to do with his teaching as with his evangelism. The pioneer of Christian missions fulfilled the commission of the Lord Jesus to 'make disciples of all nations.' To him the salvation of men was the beginning point of Christian life, not the climax. We do well to study his example in order to improve the efficiency of our service for the Lord. There is a solid biblical base in Paul's teaching ministry from which we can learn. We will look at some of the important aspects of this ministry in the following pages, especially those that touch principles applicable to missions today.

The Place of Teaching in the Missionary Strategy of Paul

The general strategy of Paul's missionary activity is clearly stated in Acts 14:21–23:

> 'And after they had preached the gospel to that city and had made many disciples, they returned to Lystra and to Iconium and to Antioch, strengthening the souls of the disciples, encouraging them to continue in the faith, and saying, "Through many tribulations we must enter the kingdom of God." And when they had appointed elders for them in every church, having prayed with fasting, they commended them to the Lord in whom they had believed.'

This took place near the end of his first missionary journey with Barnabas. For about two years they had been in the vicinity of four cities in the Roman province of Galatia. We know them as Lystra, Iconium, Derbe and Pisidian Antioch, located in what is today south central Turkey. What Paul and Barnabas did there is typical of their missionary work. In terms of missionary strategy three things stand out clearly. First, there was an evangelistic thrust. 'They preached the gospel to that city and made many disciples.' Initially they communicated the good news of salvation as widely as possible. Those that responded were called disciples. That is evangelism.

Secondly, there was the teaching process. Note the words, 'They returned strengthening the souls of the disciples, encouraging them to continue in the faith.' Paul and Barnabas worked at teaching the new believers the great truths of the Word of God so that they would be strong in the faith. That is training, and it is the emphasis of this study.

Thirdly, there was the establishment of an indigenous local church. Our passage says, 'When they had appointed elders for them in every church, . . . they commended them to the Lord in whom they had believed.' The evangelized and trained believers were formed into local assemblies with appointed elders. Thus Paul and Barnabas could leave them in the relative security of a viable local church. We will examine this at a later stage. Let us return for our present study to the apostle Paul as a teacher.

The Importance of Teaching in the Ministry of Paul

The narrative of Paul's missionary life makes it clear that he realized the importance of well-taught disciples. He knew that without adequate training the believers could not stand in a secular world, the churches would not be able to continue, and the whole Christian movement would falter. Well-taught and trained believers were vital to the life of the early church.

The importance of teaching cannot be over-emphasized. God designed it as something essential to the believer's spiritual development and service. Just as the learning/teaching process is essential to the development of man's social culture, so it is equally important to his spiritual development. Learning is defined as, 'personal development toward maturity.' Teaching is that which provides for and encourages effective learning. Missionary teaching provides for and encourages believers to understand and apply the Word of God.

Teaching is necessary for several purposes. One of these is to bring the believer to an intelligent understanding of God and His ways. 'And this is eternal life that they may know Thee the only true God' (John 17:3). Knowing God involves the learning/teaching process. Another purpose for which teaching is necessary is for personal growth toward the likeness of Christ. The Word of God is both milk and meat to the Christian. The learning/teaching process is the means for ingesting this spiritual food. A third purpose for which teaching is necessary is in learning to serve God, using the Word as a tool. A fourth purpose is to train effective witnesses for the growth of the church.

Many religions stress forms more than content. The worshipper performs a set of

duties and acts which are his main contribution
to religious observance. Christianity's emphasis is on truth and the worshipper must understand and apply it. It is because Christianity is
more content than form oriented that teaching
is so essential to its growth. Teaching is the
guardian of the faith.

Paul's Role as a Teacher

His Training for the Role of Teacher

Teaching was one of Paul's primary roles. From
the age of fourteen he was trained as a teacher of
the Law. He had come from Tarsus to Jerusalem
to study under Gamaliel. His sharp mind and
gifted personality were ideally suited to his
training. He emerged as a leading teacher of the
Pharisees in Jerusalem shortly after Pentecost.
The powerful witness of the new Christians
soon started to have an impact on his thinking.
Many were forsaking orthodox Judaism to
acknowledge Jesus as Messiah. Christian leaders such as Stephen were debating with Jews in
the various synagogues. Paul as a teacher of the
Pharisees, no doubt was one who opposed
them, but he could not resist the wisdom and
power of Stephen's arguments. They were like
goads prodding his academic mind ever closer
to acknowledging Jesus as Messiah.

The crisis came as Paul lay prostrate in the dust of the Damascus road. There he submitted to the claims of Jesus as Messiah and Lord. Paul the leader of the Pharisees became Paul the follower of Jesus. His teaching role, however, did not change. While still in Damascus, he was already 'Confounding the Jews . . . by proving that Jesus was the Christ' (Acts 9:22). Paul disappears for some years from the biblical record except for visits he made to Arabia and a fourteen-day visit to Jerusalem. When he reappears in Acts 11, he had come to Antioch at the request of Barnabas and taught considerable numbers. He was still teaching. In chapter thirteen when prophets and teachers met for prayer and fasting, Paul was among them (Acts 13:1–3). He was known as a teacher in that city. In that capacity he was sent forth with the gospel, and he taught it in the synagogues of Cyprus and South Galatia.

His Teaching Role as an Evangelist

As his evangelistic teaching bore fruit in the lives of converts, Paul continued his teaching role in confirming and strengthening the new believers in the faith. The role of teacher/trainer became the dominant role in his life. Every evangelistic effort was followed by an emphasis on building up the new believers. Sometimes he was driven out of town sooner than he planned, but even then he tried to leave strong believers as teachers. Then he himself sought to return to reinforce their teaching. When this was not practical, he wrote teaching letters to the different congregations and individuals.

His Teaching Role Through Letters

The letters of Paul form a significant part of our New Testament. His role as teacher shines in all of them. Romans is a carefully reasoned doctrinal statement of the gospel. The Corinthian letters deal with order in the local church and the progress of ministry. Galatians and the Thessalonian letters deal with issues which had arisen and needed clear answers. Paul gave them. Some of the letters handled great and lofty themes as do Ephesians and Colossians. Almost every letter applies truth to the practical everyday life of the believers. Paul was at his best as a teacher in the declaration and application of truth. Most of his letters begin with the doctrinal statement of truth and end with its application in the life of the individual, the family, and the church. Paul's pastoral letters are in the teaching mode to younger men who needed encouragement and advice. At the very end of his life Paul wrote to Timothy and warned him to be on guard against those like Alexander who opposed his teaching (2 Tim. 4:15). Paul's role as a teacher is as clear as any role in his life.

Paul's Goals as a Teacher

Teaching People to Believe in Christ

As a teacher/trainer Paul had definitive goals in mind. When he taught, he set out to accomplish these. We shall note four major goals which Paul had before him in his teaching ministry. The first of these was to so effectively teach the gospel, that men and women would be saved. We have noted before that as Paul entered the cities of the Greek world, he found the synagogues and sought opportunity to teach the gospel there. His hope was that the Jews, proselytes, and God-fearers who made up the congregations would respond by acknowledging Jesus as Messiah and by believing in Him as the crucified and risen Saviour. Paul's arrival in Corinth is typical. Acts 18:4 tells us, 'He was reasoning in the synagogue every Sabbath and trying to persuade Jews and Greeks.' At this city he was actively testifying that Jesus was the Christ (Acts 18:5).

In time the synagogue authorities evicted him, but he continued teaching both Jews and Gentiles in the house of a man called Titius Justus who lived next door. As a result, many believed including the leader of the synagogue named Crispus. Paul then stayed in Corinth for eighteen months teaching the Word of God among them (Acts 18:11). It was a ministry of

teaching the gospel in an orderly, reasoned
fashion. God honoured this ministry with many
souls. Some years later he wrote to Timothy
about this, saying, 'I was appointed a preacher
and an apostle . . . as a teacher of the Gentiles in
faith and truth' (1 Tim. 2:7). Perhaps we could
learn from Paul as a teacher of the gospel. It may
be that we have over-emphasized the 'rescue-
mission approach' or the 'crusade approach,'
looking for an immediate response, to the detri-
ment of our evangelism. Perhaps in our hurry to
make converts by preaching, we fail to make
disciples by teaching.

Teaching the Believers to be Mature in Christ

The second goal Paul had in his teaching
ministry was the personal maturity of
believers. His teaching purpose extended from
the point of their conversion toward growth in
Christian character. This goal was attained by
focus on the person of Christ. They would
learn to know Him. They would learn to be like
Him. They would learn to be protected from
error concerning Him. Paul's teaching goal was
to present every man complete (mature) in
Christ. Central to this theme is the passage in
Colossians 1:28–29:

'And we proclaim Him, admonishing every man
and teaching every man with all wisdom, that

we may present every man complete in Christ.
And for this purpose also I labour, striving
according to His power which mightily works
within me.'

Paul knew that maturity in Christ necessitated
knowing Him. He kept this as a personal goal
himself right to the end of his life. From prison
in Rome he wrote to the Philippian believers,
'That I may know Him. . . . Not that I have . . .
already become complete, but I press on . . .
toward the goal for the prize of the upward call
of God in Christ Jesus' (Phil. 3:10–14). In verse
eight he calls it 'the surpassing value of knowing Christ Jesus my Lord.' Paul had this goal,
not only for himself, but for those he taught.
Phillips paraphrases[1] the Colossian passage,
'We teach everyone we can all that we know
about Him, so that, if possible, we may bring
every man up to his full maturity in Jesus Christ.
This is what I am working at all the time with all
the strength that God gives me.'

He Taught His Students to Know Christ

Maturity in Christ also necessitated being like
Him in character. Christian character is, in
essence, Christ's character. Believers are to

---

[1] J.B. Phillips, *New Testament*.

grow into the likeness of Christ. Paul spent a
major part of his ministry in teaching this to his
converts. They were to be changed into the
image of Christ, progressively growing into
His likeness (2 Cor. 3:18). Paul's ministry to
believers aimed at change in their behaviour
and attitude. Paul taught the Colossians, 'As
you have therefore received Christ Jesus the
Lord, so walk in Him, having been firmly
rooted and now being built up in Him' (Col.
2:6–7). That is to behave like Christ. He taught
the Philippians, 'Have this attitude in yourselves which was also in Christ Jesus . . . He
humbled Himself by becoming obedient to the
point of death, even death on a cross.' That is to
think like Christ.

In addition to the inward aspect of behaving
and thinking like Christ, Paul taught his
converts to outwardly act like Christ toward
others. The third chapter of Colossians has one
of many passages on the subject. Note the
words in Colossians 3:11–14:

> 'A renewal in which . . . Christ is all and in all. And
> so . . . put on a heart of compassion, kindness,
> humility, gentleness and patience; bearing with
> one another and forgiving each other . . . just as
> the Lord forgave you. . . . And beyond all these
> things put on love which is the perfect bond of
> unity.'

He Taught Believers to Express Christ in Their Actions Toward Each Other

Another subject Paul emphasized in teaching believers to be mature was the danger of error regarding the person of Christ. Besides knowing Him and becoming like Him, they were to beware of anything beside Him. Paul's letters are full of warnings about everything which is not Christocentric.

> 'See to it that no one takes you captive through philosophy and empty deception according to the tradition of men, according to the elementary principles of the world, rather than according to Christ. For in Him all the fullness of Deity dwells in bodily form, and in Him you have been made complete (Col. 2:8–10).'

Again and again he reminds believers of the ever-present dangers of three anti-Christian philosophies, legalism, mysticism, and asceticism. He calls the teachers of such philosophies 'savage wolves' and warns the elders of Ephesus to carefully guard the flock (Acts 20:28–29).

Teaching Believers to Function in the Body of Christ

We have thus far discussed two of Paul's purposes in teaching: first, teaching people to

believe in Christ, and second, teaching believers
to be mature in Christ. Paul's third purpose was
teaching believers to function in the body of
Christ. Believers in the New Testament are seen
both as members of the universal body
composed of all believers, and also as part of a
local body or church. Paul taught believers to
function properly as part of a group, never as
isolated individuals. Their body-life was very
important. It was part of the training process.
He consistently united new Christians into a
local fellowship. Then he taught that group to
function so as to be strong.

In the central passage on Paul's missionary
strategy already discussed, Paul was at pains to
confirm, or strengthen, the souls of the disciples
(Acts 14:22). In every place where people
believed on that first missionary journey, Paul
and Barnabas returned to strengthen them. The
word 'strengthen' means to 'make to lean
upon'. Paul's purpose for these groups of
believers was to strengthen them by getting
them corporately to lean upon the great truths
of Christ and the gospel. Corporate instruction
was the means he used. God provided gifted
teachers in the local church to further this function. The elders in every local church were to be
'able to teach' among their other qualifications.

Paul taught them the priestly functions of
worship and prayer. These had marked the New
Testament congregations from the beginning

(Acts 2:42). Paul also taught them the servant functions of loving and caring for one another. Just as each member of a physical body serves the other members, so the members of a spiritual body are to act for the good of the whole body. Paul taught them to overcome relational problems. The ever-present triumvirate of the world, the flesh, and the Devil incessantly wars against the church of God, often through inter-personal problems among believers. Finally, Paul taught them to grow qualitatively as well as quantitatively. Nine of Paul's thirteen letters are directed to churches. In every one of them Paul teaches them to improve the quality of their lives in the context of the church.

Paul's aim in teaching the churches was to strengthen them. We have already noted this on his first missionary journey (Acts 14:22). The same word 'strengthen' is used again on his second missionary journey when he strengthened the churches in Cilicia and Syria (Acts 15:41). Some years later on his third journey he was still doing the same thing. Luke records that, 'He passed successively through the Galatian region and Phrygia strengthening all the disciples' (Acts 18:23).

Teaching Believers to Function as Witnesses in the World

Paul's fourth purpose as a teacher/trainer was to prepare believers for their function in the world as witnesses. The local churches he planted were not to be ends in themselves, but bases for outreach to the community and the world. Paul trained believers to imitate his evangelistic zeal. The Thessalonian church is an example of this. He congratulated them saying, 'You became imitators of us and of the Lord, having received the word in much tribulation with the joy of the Holy Spirit. . . . For the word of the Lord has sounded forth from you not only in Macedonia and Achaia, but also in every place your faith toward God has gone forth' (1 Thess. 1:6–8).

In following Paul's example of evangelism, their witness had been effective not only in their own province of Macedonia, but also in more distant places. Their outreach involved opposition and suffering, but in spite of this they did it with much joy. They repeated what they knew Paul had experienced in bringing the gospel to them. Having learned well from Paul, they did not shrink from opposition and persecution as they witnessed to their own countrymen (1 Thess. 2:13–15).

Teaching Leaders to Function Effectively

The final purpose of Paul as a teacher/trainer was to prepare leaders to carry on and expand the functions that he had been performing. Timothy is the outstanding example of this aspect of Paul's ministry. On his second missionary journey passing through Lystra, Paul found Timothy as a committed disciple who was well spoken of by believers there (Acts 16:1–2). Paul and Silas asked him to join them, and from that point on Timothy was closely associated with Paul. He was carefully trained by Paul in the Word of God and in all aspects of the ministry. Timothy became an active leader in the early church, particularly in Ephesus.

Paul refers to Timothy as his beloved son and as his true child in the faith (1 Tim. 1:2; 2 Tim. 1:2). Paul taught him as a wise father. He instructed him in every aspect of Christian discipleship and leadership. The teacher/disciple relationship is clearly expressed in the second letter to Timothy.

> But you followed my teaching, conduct, faith, patience, love, perseverance, persecutions, and sufferings such as happened to me at Antioch, at Iconium, and at Lystra; what persecutions I endured, and out of them all the Lord delivered me! And indeed, all who desire to live godly in Christ Jesus will be persecuted. But evil men and impostors will proceed from bad to worse, deceiving and being deceived. You, however, continue in the things you have learned and become convinced of, knowing from whom you have learned them (2 Tim. 3:10–14).

Timothy was to pass on those things which he had learned from Paul. Paul's objective was that Timothy train others as he himself had been trained. He wrote to him, 'You therefore, my son, be strong in the grace that is in Christ Jesus. And the things which you have heard from me in the presence of many witnesses, these entrust to faithful men, who will be able to teach others also' (2 Tim. 2:1–2). Paul's training objective was to produce leaders who could reproduce more leaders. This is, no doubt, one of the important keys to his success.

Timothy was not the only leader Paul trained. Based on the implications we have in the New Testament record, men such as Titus, Epaphras, and Epaphroditus seem to have been equally trained. Women such as Lydia and Priscilla became disciples and owed much to the teaching of the Apostle. He was constantly enlarging their capacities and urging them to realize their full potential. Paul rejoiced when they could lead where he had once led. Like other leaders he no doubt found many things he could do better than they in the beginning. But he took the time to train them and then to hand over the responsibility. He instructs Timothy how to help the church in Ephesus, rather than doing it directly himself. It was the same with Titus on the island of Crete.

Paul's Curriculum As a Teacher

The whole subject of Paul as a teacher/trainer makes it imperative that consideration be given to what he taught. If we too want to produce the Timothys and the Lydias, then we should study what he taught them. If we want to reproduce churches like those in Philippi and Ephesus, then careful attention should be given to Paul's teaching ministry in those cities. What were his sources? What subjects did he teach? Where did he find an appropriate model? His curriculum or course of study is therefore of great interest to those of us who follow him.

The Sources He Used

There were several sources Paul used for teaching material. First, of course, there were the Scriptures of the Old Testament. These were available to Paul in both Greek and Hebrew. His years of study under Gamaliel had made him a competent authority in their use and interpretation. He used them extensively as he sought to persuade Jews and God-fearers that Jesus was the Christ. For an example of his use of Scripture one should study his message in Antioch of Pisidia (Acts 13:13–50). Five different quotations from the Psalms and from the prophets Isaiah and Habakkuk are used as source material. This was at the beginning of his ministry, and throughout, his biblically-based teaching is consistently emphasized. The record of the book of Acts ends with Paul in Rome still using the Scriptures to explain why God was reaching out to Gentiles (Acts 28:26–27).

Romans is Paul's definitive statement of the truth of the gospel and is literally sprinkled with passages of the Old Testament Scriptures to make his points. He begins with the declaration that the gospel of God concerning the redemptive work of Christ was 'promised beforehand through His prophets in the Holy Scriptures' (Rom. 1:2). More than half of all the Old Testament quotations Paul used in his writings are found in Romans. His curriculum focused on the Scriptures.

Another source Paul used in teaching was his own experience with the Lord Jesus Christ. Several times over in the book of Acts he either relates his conversion or his subsequent experiences with the Lord. In his letters there are repeated autobiographical allusions and references. Paul experienced the truth he was teaching. It was never a mere academic presentation of fact. His relationship with the living Christ was a vital part of what he communicated to individuals and churches.

Paul's knowledge of the life and ministry of Jesus provided him with another important source. Although he had never personally seen or heard the Lord Jesus during His life on earth,

Paul had an extensive knowledge of much that Jesus said and did. He had heard Stephen's masterful arguments. Ananias, the disciple in Damascus, had shared Christ with him. Peter and Barnabas had related much of their knowledge concerning Christ. No doubt many others provided authentic accounts for Paul, not the least of whom was Luke who travelled extensively with him and wrote the longest of the Gospels. Luke's contribution to Paul's knowledge of the Lord Jesus must have been great. Paul used what he knew of the Lord Jesus as his primary theme in teaching. To the Corinthians he wrote, 'I determined to know nothing among you except Jesus Christ and Him crucified' (1 Cor. 2:2). To the Colossians he wrote, 'And we proclaim Him . . . teaching every man with all wisdom that we may present every man complete in Christ' (Col. 1:28).

Another important source of Paul's curriculum was directly revealed truth. Paul received from the Lord much that had not been previously revealed. Some of the great New Testament truths concerning the grace of God, the church and the church age, the coming of Christ for His own, etc. were given by the inspiration of God to Paul. These truths were included in his writings as well as in his teaching ministry. They are available to us because we have his writings in the New Testament.

The remaining source of Paul's teaching material was the ministry of the Holy Spirit in him in taking the things of Christ and showing them to him. There was also the natural wisdom that he had as leader of men. Paul used carefully all the sources available to him and applied them to his ministry.

The Subjects He Taught

With clear goals in view, Paul taught a curriculum designed to meet them. The goals, as we have seen, were personal maturity in Christ, corporate maturity in the church, witness to the world, and leadership training. In general his curriculum was the Word of God and the God of the Word. Paul understood that it was of primary importance that believers be built up in the Word of God. In his farewell address to the elders of the Ephesian church he said, 'And now I commend you to God and to the Word of His grace which is able to build you up and to give you the inheritance among all those who are sanctified (Acts 20:32).' When he moved to the city of Corinth and began to see people respond to the gospel, Luke records that, 'Paul began devoting himself completely to the Word, solemnly testifying to the Jews that Jesus was the Christ.... And he settled there a year and six months, teaching the Word of God among them' (Acts 18:5, 11).

In addition to the truth of the Word, Paul also emphasized the character of God and His Son. Paul presented God as 'The King, eternal, immortal, invisible, the only God ... who alone possesses immortality and dwells in unapproachable light, whom no man has seen or can see' (1 Tim. 1:17; 6:16). Even more specifically Paul teaches the character of the Lord Jesus Christ in literally dozens of passages. Christ is described as 'the image of the invisible God, the first-born of all creation. . . . By Him all things were created. . . . He is before all things, and in Him all things hold together. He is also the head of the body, the church. . . . For it was the Father's good pleasure for all the fullness to dwell in Him, and through Him to reconcile all things to Himself' (Col. 1:15–20). Paul emphasized the great events in the life of Christ from His incarnation to His ascension and their importance in the whole scope of Christian doctrine and practice. The glories of Christ shine in Romans as Paul leads them through the whole doctrine of salvation and justification by faith. In Ephesians he expounds the great truth of the church as the Body of Christ. To the Thessalonians he emphasizes the truth of coming things in the plan of God. These are major examples from many.

In the area of the human will Paul teaches continually how believers should respond to God. They are to commit themselves to Him as a living sacrifice. They are to be instant in prayer. Their worship is centred in the Lord Jesus Christ. They are to be controlled by the Spirit. They are to purify themselves from everything that contaminates the body and the spirit. They are to serve the living and true God. In one other area of human personality he taught that the truth in their minds and the obedience of their wills were to be balanced by the control of their emotions. Paul taught them to respond to God in praise, and song, to rejoice with those who rejoice, and to weep with those who weep (Rom. 12:15). But the emotions were not to be the master. They were to be used to the glory of God as a vehicle of expression and were always to be under control (Gal. 5:23).

In the area of the corporate growth of the church Paul had a great deal to teach. The church needed purity. It needed some structure. It needed leadership. It had to be taught to resolve problems. It was also taught the principles of true worship. Paul taught them to baptize new converts as an outward declaration of their faith. He had a special revelation from God to institute the Lord's supper of remembrance as part of the function of the church (1 Cor. 11:23–30). All nine of the letters to churches contain a variety of instructions to help them grow into corporate maturity. Such teaching was paramount in the thinking of the apostle Paul.

The witness to the world was another emphasis of Paul's teaching. He was most concerned that the message of the gospel be communicated accurately to unbelievers. Christians must have a good report to those that are without. They were to shine as lights in the world, holding forth the Word of Life (Phil. 2:15–16). Paul trained people to be witnesses. He exhorted Timothy to do the work of an evangelist. Paul saw unbelievers as those who were perishing because the god of this world has blinded the minds of men. He clearly saw the awfulness of the judgement of God; and knowing the terror of the Lord, he sought to persuade the unsaved to believe. He carefully taught the gospel.

The Model He Used

One further area in Paul's teaching curriculum deserves attention. We have looked at his sources and at the subjects he taught. Now we will note the model he used. Good teaching makes use of models. Paul had the perfect model, Christ Himself, and made use of Him in his teaching. He could use Christ the model in his teaching because he used Christ as his own ideal. To be like Christ in attitude, activity, and in character was a personal goal for Paul. 'For me to live is Christ,' he said (Phil. 1:21). He wanted to know Christ better so that he would follow His steps more closely. Likeness to

Christ was the measure of his attainment. He included himself with others who had been gifted 'for the equipping of the saints for the work of service, to the building up of the body of Christ, until we all attain to . . . the knowledge of the Son of God' and [note this!] 'to the measure of the stature which belongs to the full-ness of Christ' (Eph. 4:12–13). Christ was the standard by which he could measure his progress in godliness.

Not only did Paul strive for Christ-likeness, he taught others to strive for it as well. To the Galatians he said, 'I labour until Christ is formed in you' (Gal. 4:19). It was a goal of his teaching ministry, that believers should be conformed to the image of God's Son (Rom. 8:29). He wanted to 'present every man complete in Christ' (Col. 1:29). Christ was the example of Christian humility. 'Have this attitude in yourselves which was also in Christ Jesus who . . . taking the form of a bond-servant . . . He humbled Himself by becoming obedient to the point of death, even death on a cross' (Phil. 2:5–8).

He taught believers to be identified with Christ, in death to the old ways and in resurrec-tion life to the new ways (Rom. 6). They were to be strong in the grace that is in Christ Jesus (2 Tim. 2:1). They were to demonstrate the peace of Christ (Col. 3:15). They were to display the faith and love which are in Christ (2 Tim. 1:13). They were indwelt by the Spirit of Christ whose ministry it is to make them like Him.

They were to walk in love just as Christ had loved them (Eph. 5:2). Husbands were to love their wives 'as Christ also loved the church and gave Himself up for her' (Eph. 5:25). The Lord Jesus in His moral perfection was the model for teaching Christian living.

The model of Christ was Paul's personal standard, as well as the theme of Christian life teaching. Note finally that it was also a theme of his prayer life. The prayer in Ephesians 3 is a great one.

'I bow my knees before the Father, from whom every family in heaven and on earth derives its name, that He would grant you, according to the riches of His glory, to be strengthened with power through His Spirit in the inner man; so that Christ may dwell in your hearts through faith, and that you being rooted and grounded in love, may be able to comprehend with all the saints what is the breadth and length and height and depth, and to know the love of Christ which surpasses knowledge, that you may be filled up to all the fullness of God.' (Eph. 3:14–19).

In this great prayer Paul prays that they might be intensely aware of the fullness of the love of Christ and that they might emulate it by being rooted and grounded in it. The model of Christ

and His love was constantly before Paul in his
prayer life.

Paul's Methods in Teaching

Paul was not only a 'man for all seasons,' he was
a man for all methods. Flexibility marked his
methodology. The words he used in his teaching ministry give some indication of this. At
least five words are used by Paul in his teaching
vocabulary which indicate a breadth of instruction methods; teaching by catechism, teaching
by instruction, teaching by confrontation,
teaching by discipline, and teaching by rein-
forcement. He was a teacher par excellence and
applied various forms of teaching to accomplish his goals. Like the Lord Jesus, he had a
wide ministry with all who would listen and a
more individual ministry with those marked for
special instruction.

Public Lecture as a Means for Gospel Persuasion

Paul had remarkable success in the use of the
public lecture method as a means for gospel
persuasion. He began by using the local synagogues as a forum where both Jews and
interested Gentiles were usually gathered.
Within a short time his teaching had caused a

division of opinion and Paul was looking for another place to teach. In Corinth it was the house of a man called Titius Justus (Acts 18:7). In Ephesus it was a school building which he rented in the afternoons called the school of Tyrannus (Acts 19:9). Here he was 'reasoning daily' with any and all who would listen to the gospel he preached. No doubt the word 'reasoning' implies that there was time for discussion and questions from his hearers. This method of public lecture and discussion proved effective in Ephesus and the province of Asia.

Church Teaching Method for Instruction in Christian Life and Doctrine

Another method employed by Paul was the church teaching method for instruction in Christian life and doctrine. He used this method with groups of believers who were in the process of forming a local church and with those whose local church was already established. He sought to indoctrinate believers with the great truths of the faith and to instruct them as to how they were to behave as believers. A brief survey of Paul's teaching activity in Acts will show this in place after place. The churches in Lystra, Iconium, and Antioch were strengthened by Paul's teaching (Acts 14:22). Others in Cilicia and Syria were taught in the same manner (Acts 15:41). In Corinth he carefully instructed them for eighteen months (Acts 18:11). In Troas, even on a brief visit, he took the opportunity to instruct the church until late at night (Acts 20:7). The three years in Ephesus were used to teach the increasing number of believers 'about the kingdom of God' (Acts 19:8). These examples emphasize the importance of teaching in the local church as practiced by the apostle.

Select Group Method for Leadership Preparation

The third teaching method was select group training for leadership preparation. As soon as a viable assembly of believers was forming, Paul was looking for those who might be God's choice for leadership there. They were generally his own converts from areas where he evangelized. He aimed to stay in each place long enough to see their maturity as leaders and elders (Acts 14:23). This required that he prepare these men for the leadership in the local church. The clearest look at this principle at work is in regard to the establishment of the church at Ephesus. In visiting these men at the end of his third missionary journey, he reminded them that for a three-year period, he had been with them the whole time teaching them from house to house (Acts 20:17–20). He had taught them the whole purpose of God. He had admonished each one with tears. He warned them of the coming of false teachers who would draw away followers. He prepared them for their role as elders in the local church to 'shepherd the church of God' which was valuable beyond compare because it had been purchased with His own blood (Acts 17:20–35).

Individual Apprenticeship Method for Missionary Training

The final teaching method Paul used was the one-on-one apprenticeship method for missionary training. Paul was on the lookout for other men to do the kind of missionary work he was doing. For this purpose he selected men who had potential and invited them to join him and the missionary band. Timothy is the outstanding example of this. He had evidently been converted at Lystra. He then was noticed by Paul on the second missionary journey and was asked to join the evangelistic group. Paul trained him for the next several years to be the kind of missionary he was.

The two letters to Timothy give some insights into the relationship of these two men. Paul had committed to Timothy the whole counsel of God as he understood it. He impressed the younger man that it was a sacred trust which was to be kept pure and safe. 'O Timothy, guard what has been entrusted to you,' he wrote to him (1 Tim. 6:20). The second emphasis in Paul's training of Timothy was to urge him to pass on what he knew to others. 'The things which you have heard from me . . . these entrust to faithful men who will be able to teach others also' (2 Tim. 2:2). The main point in this section is that faithful men were selected and trained for the ministry. Paul thus used the same apprentice method practiced by the Lord Jesus with His disciples.

Paul's teaching and training ministry was not limited to men. It is evident that he taught women with the expectation that they would take places of usefulness. Lydia of Philippi was one of these who responded to the teaching of Paul (Acts 16:14–15). Priscilla and her husband Aquila were active in the ministry and are mentioned several times in four books of the New Testament. Philip's four daughters were prophetesses (Acts 21:9). Phoebe was a 'servant of the church' at Cenchrea (Rom. 16:1). Four more women come in for special mention in Romans sixteen. Paul had an interest in training them for their role in serving God.

Paul used these methods in his teaching – from the public platform to individual discipleship. The four methods are progressively more select regarding the audience and more intense regarding the teaching.

Contemporary Examples

The four growth models used in this study all teach us the importance of discipling of new believers. In Durban, South Africa the most helpful ministry in which we were involved was an evening Bible school connected with the growing number of assemblies being formed. The Zulus recognized their need for teaching if they were to be available to God for service. They willingly delayed an evening meal by several hours and came straight from their jobs in the city to the assembly building where the studies were held. Some women came, but they were limited by the factors of distance and danger. For two hours, two evenings a week they listened, compared Scriptures, took notes, asked questions and simply enjoyed the Word of God. We did surveys of the Bible, doctrinal studies, Christian life studies; usually two sessions with two subjects per evening. Other missionaries came from as far as a hundred miles away to give variety. Then God raised up gifted Zulu men to teach sessions. The majority of the men who came were younger and therefore the future leaders in the churches. This proved to be true.

On another continent and a generation later my son Jim Fleming started a similar programme in Bogota. The Bogota assembly work had begun with the vision and work of Brian Killins. It grew to the point where he saw the need for help and one of those who came was Jim (Jaime). His vision was for teaching and he began a programme called Project Paul. It is being held in five of the assembly buildings each week and taught by a number of men, both Colombian and missionary. Over one hundred and fifty men and women are currently studying the Scriptures in five different assemblies with others coming from places where they are not currently meeting. Leadership is emerging. The Sunday teaching and preaching is improving. Problems are being solved more biblically. And, best of all, the mind set of these men and women is being founded on the Living Word, rather than on the deadly cultural values surrounding them.

In Austria where their evangelism was of necessity more personal and low key the approach was different. Almost all converts faced some form of persecution. The Schneiders did not invite any to the church meetings until after they were saved. This meant that the church meetings concentrated on doctrine, prayer, fellowship and the breaking of bread (Acts 2:42). The centre and focus of their teaching is the church. Schneider says 'The monthly men's meetings will become the main avenue for training the men in leadership'.

In Belgium, they emphasized teaching. Richard Haverkamp writes, 'From the moment of conversion we begin to teach the believers the great truths concerning the body of Christ, the church. They are now part of that body, which is a real privilege, but also a responsibility' He goes on to say, 'Our responsibility as leaders is *not* to do the work for the believers, but to train the believers to do the work so that we can move on . . . Time is spent with some to develop their teaching gift and opportunity given to practice'.

Conclusion

As an example of missionary teaching and training, Paul is outstanding. We do well if we pay more attention to the clear record left us in the New Testament. Many missionaries and workers have allowed themselves to be over-involved in less important forms of service and have missed the opportunity to train their converts for life and for the life of the church. Biblical missions must lay strong emphasis on teaching: teaching the gospel, teaching new converts, training leaders, and reproducing missionaries. It is remarkable that Paul accomplished these goals with no institution or formal curriculum. Many today are so obsessed with the institutional opportunities around them that they ignore the more basic opportunities for preparing other believers to serve God.

Without a doubt the mushrooming church in much of the third world has as its greatest need the establishment of well-taught Christian leaders who can teach others also. Africa, Asia, and Latin America all cry for it. Since this is a great need, the emphasis of missionaries should be toward meeting that need by producing reproducers; not just teaching, but preparing others to teach. This was a major focus in the ministry of Paul.

4

Church Planting in the Ministry of Paul

Paul's skill as a missionary is nowhere more marked than in his success as a church planter. He was an effective evangelist – hundreds came to know Christ through his preaching. He also excelled as a teacher and trainer of people. As a faithful parent trains his children so Paul brought his spiritual children to maturity. His crowning activity was that he formed churches from the believers who had been evangelized and taught. The planting of churches was the third and final step in the strategy of Pauline mission (Acts 14:21–23).

The remarkable thing is that he did it. As we examine the accomplishments of Paul and the principles underlying them, we will discover that we too can succeed. It is neither complicated nor confusing. Paul showed us how to do it. We can, under God, plant churches as he did.

Neither the power nor the principles have changed.

In our study of Paul as a missionary church planter we will look first at the concept of the church and how he gained his understanding of it. Then we will note the priority of church planting in his ministry. We will look at the local church which became the model for those he established. Finally, we will examine the principles which made his church planting so successful.

Paul's Concept of the Church as God's Institution

Before conversion Paul viewed the church as a sect of misguided Jews who had been brainwashed into thinking that Jesus of Nazareth was the Messiah and had been raised from the dead. The sight of crowds of His followers in the temple area singing His praise filled Saul with rage because he saw them as enemies of the truth and as a threat to orthodox Jewry. As a leader of the Pharisees he organized an opposition movement to eradicate those who called themselves the church. After the martyrdom of Stephen, 'Saul began ravaging the church, entering house after house; and dragging off men and women, he would put them in prison' (Acts 8:3).

After his conversion Saul's concept of the church changed. He realized that Jesus was indeed the Messiah and that the proof of this was that He had risen from the dead. Instead of persecuting the church he now sought to help its cause. He aligned himself with the disciples who were in the church and acknowledged that Jesus was the Lord and builder of His church, just as He had said to the twelve, 'I will build My church and the gates of Hades shall not over-power it' (Matt. 16:18). Saul immediately became a bold witness for Christ in Damascus until a plot against his life was discovered (Acts 9:30). He escaped with the help of other disciples and went into seclusion in Arabia (Gal. 1:7–17).

There, in Arabia, it would seem that Paul's concept of the church broadened. God made known to him by revelation those transcendent truths about the church of which he later wrote in his inspired letters. Paul became the exponent of the New Testament church as God designed it. His concept of the church includes all that God has been pleased to reveal about it. When he was a Pharisee he had thought of the church as a cancer to be removed. As a disciple he looked on the church as a brotherhood of believers in the Lord Jesus Christ. Finally as an apostle Paul saw the church as a divine organ-ism at the centre of God's plan for this age.

The Church as a Living Organism

A majority of people in our day look on the church as an institution. Paul's concept of the church is that it is an organism. Christianity in our day has largely obscured this truth with its emphasis on buildings, programmes and agencies. Christians speak of attending church rather than of being the church. Paul would have been horrified by this idea. He saw the church as a living community of believers bound together in a shared life. The word he used to describe this community means simply a gathering of people, as an assembly or congregation. It never refers to a building, a place or an organization. To Paul the church is people.

Paul used the word (ekklesia) to describe a spiritual organism at two different levels. At one level the church describes the totality of all believers in every place, a universal community. When Paul tells us that 'Christ also loved the church and gave Himself up for her,'he speaks of this universal church (Eph. 5:25). He calls it the 'body' of Christ formed by the special action of the Holy Spirit (1 Cor. 12:13). The head of the body is the Lord Jesus (Col. 1:28). The true church of God is universal and spiritual. It transcends any earthly institution or organization. It is what the Lord Himself referred to when He said, 'I will build my church' (Matt. 16:18). The universal church is growing and being built up

as believers all over the world come to Christ
(Eph. 4:12–16). The church was designed to
grow.

At another level Paul described the church as
a local community of believers who meet
together in the name of the Lord Jesus. These
local congregations of believers meet in one
place and are often referred to by Paul (e.g. the
church in Corinth, or Thessalonica, or Antioch
(Acts 13:1; 1 Cor. 1:2; 1 Thess. 1:1)). Provincial
areas such as Galatia, Asia, and Macedonia
were referred to as having a number of assemblies (churches) within them (1 Cor. 16:1, 9; 2
Cor. 8:1). The many local churches were linked
to the one universal church in that they were of
the same spiritual essence. Especially in relation
to Christ the local churches were like miniatures
of the universal church. Paul used the same
metaphors to describe both of them. When the
church is described as a body, Christ is the
all-wise head of the body. When described as a
flock, Christ is the shepherd. When described as
a temple, Christ is the object of worship. Local
churches were to acknowledge and to demonstrate the supremacy of Christ in their assemblies as the head of the body, the loving
bridegroom, the feeding and leading shepherd,
and the object of worship.

Paul looked at the local church as a dynamic
organism. Its life was that of Christ Himself. Its
unity was maintained through His presence. Its

direction and purpose were from Him. Paul
expected to plant these organisms wherever
he went with the gospel. He nurtured them
with a view to growth both qualitatively and
quantitatively. He established them so that they
could thrive and grow in the cultural setting of
the community. He encouraged them to
reproduce themselves in the surrounding
communities and, by extension, in distant
places. Living organisms grow and reproduce if
they are healthy. Paul viewed the churches in
this way.

The Church as a Structured Community

Paul's concept of the church as a living
organism must not be construed to mean that it
was formless, a mere blob of living cells. He saw
the church as having form and structure. In
creation biological organisms all have highly
complex structures. One of the wonders of the
life sciences is this very complexity. The deeper
scientific investigation is able to penetrate, the
more the awesome wonder of God's design is
revealed. Just as every living thing in creation
has order and form, so the church, which is a
spiritual organism, has order and form. For a
church planter like Paul it was important to
have the form clearly in mind, because it was
his responsibility to set the pattern in the
beginning.

Paul looked at the local church in Corinth as God's building. It had design, order, and structure (1 Cor. 3:9, 19). He looked at himself as the master builder of that local church structure and others were to be involved with him in the building process. There was the warning that each builder of the local church must be careful as to how they build; structure was important and every church planter should strive to follow the pattern.

Of what did the New Testament local church structure consist? How do we justify the bewildering array of complicated structures in the church today? Most of them emerge from history and culture more than they do from the Scripture. Our interest here has only to do with Paul's understanding of church order as revealed in the New Testament. The fact that he says little about it is taken by some to indicate that it is relatively unimportant or that it was so natural that he did not need to give much instruction about it. In my view, the reason for relatively little Pauline teaching on church organization is that God intended it to be simple and basic. The organization was to go no further than the autonomous local church.

The symbols used indicate structure. We have already mentioned the building with its plan and builder. The symbol of the body indicated order from the head and cooperation and control of all the members. The church as a household indicated headship and order. The church as a priesthood presumes ordered activity and a high priest. The truth is that there is no organism which is not organized. Order and structure are New Testament principles; there is no room in the writings of Paul for an unorganized church that exists strictly as an unstructured fellowship of believers doing their own thing.

The churches Paul had a part in planting all shared a common structure, albeit a simple one. It was no accident that those in Lystra, Philippi, Corinth, and Ephesus shared a similar pattern of organization, even though widely scattered geographically. Nor is it accidental that the structures in the planted churches were similar to the church in Antioch from which Paul and Barnabas were commended to the grace of God for the work.

Let us consider some of those features of structure which are clear. First there was a statutory authority. This came from the apostles and prophets of the New Testament church to whom God revealed His truth about the church and through whom the first churches were planted. Their understanding of church principles was later embodied in the New Testament which we now have as our authority.

Then there was government. Paul established elders in every church (Acts 14:23). He instructed Timothy clearly on the qualifications and functions of leaders in Ephesus where Timothy was at the time (1 Tim. 3). He also instructed Titus about them for the churches on Cyprus, they were to be appointed in every city on the island (Tit. 1:4–10). He wrote to the Philippian believers and included the overseers in his salutation (Phil. 1:1). Paul called together the Ephesian elders to give them some final words of instruction (Acts 20:17). Besides the elders there were deacons (servants) who served the churches in different and subordinate areas of leadership. Qualifications were given for these as well (1 Tim. 3; Tit. 1).

A third feature of Pauline church structure was that there was to be purpose and order in the meetings. The Corinthian believers met together as a local church (1 Cor. 11:18) to celebrate the Lord's supper in worship (1 Cor. 11:23) and to benefit from the spiritual gifts of the people in the church (1 Cor. 12:4). The importance of order is shown by Paul's strong language in correcting the disorders (11:27–34; 14:1–40). They met together for prayer and teaching (Acts 20:7, 20). Men and women had differing roles and there was order for these. They appear to have met on the first day of the week with ordered regularity (1 Cor. 16:2).

There was order to their giving and use of money. It was to be put aside according to the prosperity of each and then given through the local church for specified purposes (1 Cor. 16:2).

Moneys were handled by a plurality of treasurers. There was also order in the discipline of a sinning person in the fellowship (1 Cor. 5:1–13).

The Church as a Functioning Community

In Paul's mind the church was more than life and form. The local church was also to be focused on function. He saw the church as an organism designed by God to function in accomplishing God's purposes. That function was in general to glorify God. Paul states, 'To Him be the glory in the church' (Eph. 3;21). In glorifying God the church, as Paul saw it, was to function in three directions.

The first function was in relation to God, upward. The churches were gatherings for believers for worship. They were to express to God their praise, adoration, and thanksgiving. They were to acknowledge the greatness and holiness of God. They were to celebrate the Lord's supper as a vehicle for the worship and remembrance of the Lord Jesus Christ.

The second great function of the church as Paul viewed it was inward, toward its own members. They were to be built up in the faith, brought to maturity – they were to grow up. The risen Lord gave spiritual gifts such as teaching to people in the church to provide for its growth (Eph. 4:8–13). Paul in his letters gave examples of teaching truth to churches. To the church in

Rome he gave a masterful survey of the truths of salvation. To the Ephesians he explained the doctrine of the church. To the Thessalonians it was the truth of coming things.

Within this inward function there was room for admonition and discipline. The people of God need constant exhortation in terms of their walk with God and their relationship with each other. The local church provides for this. It also functions to care for the needs of its members. Some need restoration; others are weak and need strengthening.

Another side of the inner functioning of the church was that of fellowship or 'koinonia.' The local church functions so that its members share a common life. This is true in the spiritual life as well as in the social life. It even includes financial sharing. Fellowship is that which binds the Christians together.

The third great function of the church was outward toward the unbelieving world around them. Christ is building His church (Matt. 16:18). At the heart of what God is doing in this age is the fact that 'He is taking out from among the Gentiles a people for His name' (Acts 15:14). Paul taught that evangelism must be central in the function of the church. The church was not only the goal of evangelistic activity, it was the base for evangelism in the New Testament. To the Thessalonian church Paul said, 'For the word of the Lord has sounded forth from you not only in Macedonia and Achaia, but also in every place' (1 Thess. 1:8). The Roman church had great evangelistic zeal. Their faith was 'being proclaimed throughout the whole world' (Rom. 1:8) and Paul gives thanks for this. It is interesting that a by-product of Paul's two-year teaching in Ephesus was that all who lived in Asia heard the word of the Lord, both Jews and Greeks (Acts 19:10).

The Priority of Church Planting in Paul's Ministry

Having looked at the life, form, and function of the church as Paul understood it, we need to look at the relative importance of the church as an institution in his missionary strategy. What place does church planting have as compared with leading souls to Christ or teaching the Word of God? How does Paul compare it to meeting the social needs of people who may be oppressed or poor?

The record in the book of Acts from chapters nine to twenty-eight is basically the narrative of a man called Paul who was sent forth from a local church in Syrian Antioch and spent the rest of his life planting and nurturing other local churches in four Roman provinces (Galatia, Macedonia, Achaia, and Asia). We have the record of the establishment of about ten churches and mention of about ten more which seem to have directly resulted from the first ten, e.g. Colossae and Laodicea seem to have been offshoots from the Ephesus campaign. The next thirteen books in our New Testament are letters of Paul written to these same churches or to people within them. The emphasis of the New Testament record about the ministry of Paul is overwhelmingly on his activities as a church planter and leader. In this section I would like us to explore why this is. If the life and growth of the local churches were so important to Paul, then we who follow him are wise to consider why. I would like to suggest four reasons why church planting was important in Paul's missionary strategy.

The Church is Central to God's Plan for This Age

The first reason for Paul's high priority on church planting was that the church was central to God's plan for this age. The church began when the risen Lord poured out His Spirit on the day of Pentecost. During the course of the age He is 'taking from among the Gentiles a people for His name' (Acts 15:14). He has become the head of the church 'which is His body, the fullness of Him who fills all in all' (Eph. 1:23). He distributed gifts for the building up of the church (Eph. 4:8–16). When the church is complete the Lord Himself will come and take her to be with Him forever (1 Thess. 4:16, 17).

The Church is Important for the Spiritual Health of God's People

The second reason for the priority of church planting was that it is necessary for the welfare of God's people in an alien world. In His wisdom God provided for their spiritual and social needs. The church was a place for fellowship and gave a sense of belonging to Christians in a hostile world. It was a place for corporate worship and prayer as believer/priests brought their sacrifices of praise to God. It was a place for growing in grace and character. It was a place for the correction and discipline of God's children when they disobeyed Him. It was a place to serve one another.

The Church is Efficient for Worldwide Evangelism

A third reason for Paul's church planting priority is its efficiency in terms of world evangelism. God designed it so that believers would be saved, then taught to grow to maturity, and finally gathered into a local church. From the strength of the local church fellowship they were to reach out, to evangelize, teach, and plant other local churches which would then repeat the process. In society healthy babies are born, brought up to maturity, and then married. The result is that from the institution of marriage there will be more babies, who will be brought up and marry to repeat the process. When healthy churches function in this way, the result is the most efficient and satisfactory means of world evangelism. It is the key to world evangelism. It will happen both in the culture of the parent church and also cross-culturally with those who deliberately cross cultural boundaries for the sake of the gospel.

The Church is Ideal for Developing Maturity and Leadership

A fourth reason for Paul's church planting priority is that it provides the best possible growth environment for maturity and leader-ship. A healthy local church gives the new convert a balanced diet of spiritual food, a place for worship and prayers, direction for Christian service, and guidance when mistakes are made. There is a spectrum of age groups and people with whom to interact and grow. Wise leaders provide opportunity to develop gifts and to reach personal potential. It is an excellent training ground. Even in our day of specializa-tion the church remains the basic element in God's provision for Christian maturity.

The Priority of Church Planting has Important Implications for Today

The high priority for church planting has some important implications for missionaries today. They should not allow themselves to think that in our modern world church planting has been superseded by some other forms of Christian activity. There are strong pressures to put emphasis on the social needs in the world. But clearly the biblical emphasis of missions is on making disciples and forming them into churches. Others are so taken up with the technical advances of our day and the methodology of using them, that they become an end in themselves rather than tools for use in planting healthy churches. We must never lose sight of the importance of church planting.

Paul's Model for the Local Church – Antioch

Christianity was born in Jerusalem. It was there that Jesus was crucified and resurrected. It was there on the day of Pentecost that the church was founded. Jerusalem was the focal point of the movement of God. It seemed to be destined for a central place as the church grew and developed. Yet this was not to be. In the plan of God it was not Jerusalem but Antioch which became the epicentre of the evangelism explosion in the first century!

Antioch was a commercial centre on the coast of Syria. It was the third largest city in the Roman empire. Following the martyrdom of Stephen and the subsequent persecution, thousands of Christians fled from Jerusalem. A substantial group of these Jewish Christians spoke Greek, and some settled in Antioch. They began witnessing to the Gentile people around them. Then a surprising thing happened. Greek-speaking Gentiles responded to the gospel in significant numbers. Soon, for the first time in history, a church was established that was made up largely of non-Jewish believers.

The Antioch assembly grew rapidly and its influence spread with increasing effectiveness. In fact, for the next century Antioch was Christianity's most important centre. It was the springboard of the missionary travels of Paul and his team of church-planting evangelists. It can truly be said that the 'Antioch model' set the standard for the missionary thrust of early Christianity.

The Centrality of Christ

The churches Paul had established in the cities of Galatia were modelled after the church in Antioch; that is, the operating principles which formed the basis of the local church were the same. These principles did not necessarily have to do with form and method. One of these was the centrality of Christ, He was the focus of their gathering. In Antioch they became known as Christians (Christ ones) because Christ was central (Acts 11:20, 26). Another principle was the unified fellowship where their former religion, race, or status was ignored in the function of the church. The names of the leaders in Antioch indicate wide diversity in background which was no longer a dividing factor to them in the fellowship of believers (Acts 13:1).

In Antioch there was diversity of spiritual gift and freedom for its use. Prophets and teachers were using their gifts (Acts 13:1). There was spiritual vitality indicated by people praying and fasting (Acts 13;2). Plurality of leadership was another principle. Five men are seen in that position (Acts 13:1). Then there was sound teaching. Right from the beginning Barnabas was so concerned about it that he went all the way to Tarsus to bring Paul to teach them (Acts 11:25, 26).

Energetic evangelism was another principle of the assembly in Antioch. They were 'preaching the Lord Jesus' with vigour and with results (Acts 11:20, 21). They were also marked by what may be called responsible autonomy. Antioch was autonomous as an independent local church under Christ, but it was responsible in that it showed concern for the hurting believers in Judea. They sent money to them in a time of famine (Acts 11:29, 30). A final principle was that of missionary vision. In waiting upon God they were responsible to the Spirit of God as He indicated that two of their number were to leave Antioch for missionary work in other parts (Acts 13:1–3).

In tracing the record of Paul's subsequent ministry it is instructive to observe that these very principles were taught and practiced in the churches he established in the cities around the Aegean Sea such as Philippi, Thessalonica, and Corinth. In accomplishing his missionary goals Paul had a model to follow in every important aspect of mission, especially in his church-planting ministry. Antioch was the proper model because it was the first of the New Testament churches to be composed of both Jew and Gentile. It was the first church to be unconnected with the ritual of Judaism. It was geographically at the hub of world trade and commerce. Disciples were first called Christians there. The example of the New Testament church was first displayed there. Paul had the personal experience of being there, but we have the biblical record as a guide.

Other things which may seem important to us are not even mentioned in the Scripture. They are obviously not part of the biblical pattern. Whether we practice them or not will have to be decided on grounds other than biblical reference. No reference is made to the property and buildings a church may or may not have. Creeds and constitutions have no New Testament precedent. Nor has former ritual. There is no mention of central organization or headquarters, most certainly Jerusalem was not that. The use of Sunday Schools or seminaries is not proved from the New Testament any more than are para-church organizations or mission agencies. These may or may not be useful to us, but the principles as seen in the model New Testament church are fundamental and basic.

Paul's Principles of Church Planting – Ephesus

In Paul's application of the principles of church planting it will be helpful to notice his involvement in the emerging church at Ephesus. This church provides us with the most detail over the longest period of any example in the New Testament. It also provides us with a fairly clear outline of Pauline mission strategy. We will note the different stages in the development of the Ephesian church and the activities of Paul and his helpers at each stage.

The Evangelist Stage

The first stage we shall call the evangelistic stage. It really began in the mind of Paul on his second missionary journey. After strengthening the churches in the Galatian region he was burdened for the people of Asia of which Ephesus was the chief city (Acts 16:6). The year was about A.D. 50. Ephesus was a target area in Paul's thinking. At that time the Spirit of God did not allow them to go there. However, two years later at the very end of the second missionary journey, Paul in the company of Priscilla and Aquila arrived in Ephesus (Acts 18:19). He began to reason with the Jews in the synagogue as usual, but soon left for his home town of Antioch leaving Priscilla and Aquila to work in Ephesus. Evangelism evidently continued, particularly after Apollos arrived. Priscilla and Aquila detected that he had a deficiency in his knowledge so they explained the way of God more accurately to him. Apollos continued proving to the Jews that Jesus was the Christ (Acts 16:24–28).

Another year passed and Paul again arrived in Ephesus about A.D. 53. He found twelve men who had been prepared by God for salvation. They believed and were baptized in the name of the Lord Jesus and so the church was born in Ephesus. Evangelism had marked the first stage. Priscilla, Aquila, Apollos, and Paul had all been a part of the evangelistic thrust (Acts 18:18–19:8). Once there was a small group of believers meeting in the name of the Lord Jesus they formed an infant church.

The Teaching Stage

The new work in Ephesus now entered the next stage – the teaching stage. The evangelism of the first stage would not stop, but now teaching would mark the qualitative growth of the new assembly. Teaching was the basis of their understanding and practice of Scripture. Teaching was necessary for the vitality of their worship and the development of their Christian character. As in every young church, Paul and his co-workers laid heavy emphasis on the nurturing of the young believers. Its whole future in Ephesus was at stake, so this stage was vitally important. It will help to notice the biblical record of this growth.

The teaching stage began with Paul renting a school building for his teaching in the afternoons (Acts 19:9). He taught both formally in the lecture style of the classroom and informally from house to house as the needs arose (Acts 20:20). His adaptability is most instructive for those who insist on limiting their ministry to a speciality which they enjoy. Notice that Paul's attitude in teaching was 'with humility serving the Lord with tears and with trials' (Acts 20:19).

His courage too is outstanding as he continued in spite of opposition from the Jews and the civic unrest which followed (Acts 19:23–41). The personal cost to Paul was high. He relates that he had fought with wild beasts at Ephesus (1 Cor. 15:32). His helpers, Priscilla and Aquila, had risked their necks to save Paul's life there. Andronicus and Junias had also suffered imprisonment with him (Rom. 16:7). One further comment on Paul as the teaching church planter was that he was willing to work at tent making to pay the bills while ministering to the believers in Ephesus (Acts 20:33–34).

As he nurtured this young church, Paul taught a wide spectrum of subject matter. Doctrinally he taught the whole purpose of God (Acts 20:27). In terms of Christian conduct he says to them that, 'I did not shrink from declaring to you anything that was profitable' (Acts 20;20). This included exhortation (Acts 20:1) and personal admonition (Acts 20:31). It included teaching on holiness so that idols were burned (Acts 19:18, 19). Baptism also was considered important (Acts 19:5).

Elders were appointed and took their position as the shepherds of the church which was purchased with the blood of Christ. They had been made overseers by the operation of the Holy Spirit (Acts 20:28). These elders were warned of the danger of false teachers who would invade the fellowship (Acts 20:29–31).

They were taught to help the weak and to give to the poor (Acts 20:35). With such a well-rounded programme for growth it is no wonder that the Word of the Lord grew mightily (Acts 19:20).

The Indigenous Growth Stage

The evangelistic and teaching stages were followed by the indigenous growth stage. This stage in the life of the growing church may be described as the point at which the church planter is no longer needed on a continuing basis and the church can continue to grow and reproduce as a result of the resources placed there by God. It has become an indigenous local church; self-supporting, self-governing, and self-propagating. The parental care of Paul and his co-workers resulted in a viable church in Ephesus. Paul had made it a consistent policy to establish churches and then to wean them away from his own control and direction. He did this by physically leaving them so that the local leadership could effectively take control (e.g. Acts 14:21–24).

The farewell address to the elders of the Ephesian church is an excellent example of this principle. This was at the end of his third missionary journey. All Paul's subsequent contact with the church there was either by letter or by messenger. Many believe, however, from a reference in his first letter to Timothy that Paul did visit Ephesus between his two Roman imprisonments (1 Tim. 1:3). Information about the continuance of the assembly in Ephesus comes from the letter Paul wrote to them during his first imprisonment in Rome and from the two letters to Timothy who was living in Ephesus when Paul wrote them. Much later the Apostle John gives a final glimpse in Revelation, chapter three.

During the teaching stage Paul had deliberately taught them to grow by evangelism. He trained his disciples 'so that' (indicating purpose) 'all who lived in Asia heard the Word of the Lord, both Jews and Greeks' (Acts 19:10). When he left they were able to continue growing without his personal direction. Before Paul left there was a functioning body of elders which gave direction to the assembly. There was to be a continuing supply of gifts which were described as coming from the risen Lord and given for the purpose of the building up of the body of Christ (Eph. 4:10–12). The whole church was to grow up 'in all aspects into Him Who is the Head, even Christ' (Eph. 4:15).

Each member of the local body was to provide his/her share toward the body's growth, 'according to the proper working of each individual part' resulting in 'the growth of the body for the building up of itself in love' (Eph. 4:16). From his prison cell Paul wrote to

these Ephesians explaining the great mystery of
the church in the purposes of God. He emphasized the unity of the body of Christ and the love
that should mark the bride of Christ. He urged
them to walk in love and to be imitators of God.
He warned them of the subtlety and power of
Satan and counselled them to take the whole
armour of God.

Later when writing to Timothy who was in
Ephesus, he reminded him of the place of
prayer and the role of women in the church in
Ephesus (1 Tim. 2). He re-emphasized the work
and qualifications of elders and deacons in the
church there (1 Tim. 3). He warned of the
problems of the last days (1 Tim. 4).

The second letter to Timothy, who was still in
Ephesus, was written during Paul's second
imprisonment and shortly before his death. He
urged the younger man to guard the deposit of
the truth and to commit it carefully to faithful
men who would be able to teach others also
(2 Tim. 2:2). In this last contact with the
Ephesian church Paul sent greetings to Priscilla
and Aquila who had been faithful from the very
beginning.

Much later, by probably thirty years, the
Apostle John wrote to them from the prison
island of Patmos reminding them that they
had left their first love. He called on them to
repent or else they were in danger of having
the lampstand of their testimony removed

(Rev. 2:1–7). At that point the church at Ephesus passes from the biblical record. It had become one of the strongest and best of those described in the New Testament. The principles of church growth had been practiced there in each of three stages. In the evangelistic stage Ephesians had come to Christ in large numbers. The instruction stage saw a healthy growing church come to maturity. Finally they entered the indigenous growth stage to become a centre for outreach to other cities in the province of Asia. In all probability, the famed 'seven churches of Asia' were an outgrowth of the church in Ephesus. When we plant healthy local churches which give birth to other churches we are accomplishing the pattern for church growth laid down in God's Word.

Contemporary Examples

The examples of cross-cultural church growth which we have selected all understood the biblical centrality of the local church in New Testament practice. Their work was not accomplished until the church was established and indigenous. Richard Haverkamp says this about indigenous churches in Belgium, 'We have often been amazed at what God has been able to do . . . without us (missionaries) and what He can do with and through young converts. It makes one wonder whether at times

the constant presence of missionaries . . . has not
hindered the growth and development of the
young believers. The departure of the missionary may cause some anxiety, but it often has a
healthy outcome. They must now turn to the
Lord and learn to lean on Him'. Nearly thirty
indigenous churches in northern Belgium demonstrate the truth of that statement. Even if the
missionaries left today, the churches remain to
glorify God there.

The same is true of the lower Austrian
churches which are all in Austrian hands and
continue as spiritually healthy congregations
firmly planted in Austrian soil. They are
witness to the wisdom of the men and women
who tilled the soil, sowed the seed and tended
the young plants. In South Africa the Durban
assemblies were left on their own in 1976 when
the Flemings left the country. They have continued well under purely African leadership. They
hold their conferences, arrange evangelistic
meetings, discipline any that need it and sent a
promising leader to Bible School.

The assemblies in Bogota have done a particularly good job in establishing local congregations. When a congregation begins there they
lease a two storey row house and convert it to
church use. It will hold a maximum of about 150
people. When they get near that number they
think in terms of a 'hive-off' where a group of
30–40 will begin in another area. The elders will

be recognized and from there on they make the decisions. They too will lease a house and convert it for use as a church building. More people get saved and are then trained in the Word and the work of God. When they too fill their facility the same thing happens again. The various assemblies have a *junta* (leadership meeting) from the different assemblies about four times a year to plan the larger meetings and outreach. They now have fourth generation 'hive-offs', the latest of which has gone from 40 to 120 attenders in nine months. To the author this is a great model which is not dependant on missionary money and becomes indigenous very quickly.

Conclusion

The question of Borodin in the preface ought to confront us again. 'That man Paul. . . . Where do you find him today?' We have looked at the heart of Paul's ministry, evangelism, discipline and church planting as a model for every age, including our own. He discovered the essentials of missions and practiced them right through his ministry. We have also noted that there are some good contemporary examples to encourage us. There are, of course, hundreds of other such examples of faithful men and women who have stuck to the essentials. So we would answer Mr. Borodin, 'Perhaps you have not noticed Sir, but our God has placed hundreds of Pauls in this world whose collective efforts have accomplished more for the souls of men than your communist ideology has ever done'. Let us, as servants of God practice Paul's 'essentials of service'.

Bibliography

Johnstone, Patrick, Operation World, Carlisle, Cumbria, UK, OM Publishing, Paternoster Press, 1995

Allen, Roland, Missionary Methods: St Paul's or Ours?, Grand Rapids, Mi., Eerdmans, 1962.

Seamands, John T, Harvest Humanity, Wheaton Il., Victor Press, 1988

Kane, J. Herbert, Understanding Christian Missions, Grand Rapids, Mi., Baker Book House, 1974

Larkin, William J, and Williams, Joel F. Mission in the New Testament, An Evangelical Approach, Monrovia, Ca., Marc Publications, 1998

Peters, George W. A Biblical Theology of Missions, Chicago, Moody Press, 1972

Adney, David H. The Unchanging Commission, Chicago, Inter-Varsity Press, 1955

Haverkamp, Richard, 'God is at Work in Belgium', Missions (June, 1988) pp. 3

Phillips, J. B. 'New Testament in Modern English', Fount, 1995

Appendix

Echoes of Service

Some readers may be unfamiliar with Echoes of Service. Echoes has functioned as a missionary service group since 1872, based for most of that time in Bath. It was originally the vision of Dr John Maclean and Henry Groves, whose father Anthony Norris Groves had served as a missionary in Baghdad and subsequently in India. Groves' father is sometimes referred to as the father of faith missions and came from the same church background, the Christian Brethren as George Muller, his brother in law. Henry Groves' concern was to record the missionary work of those who were serving God in different parts of the world with no formal links to any of the existing missionary societies. They were simply depending on God to guide them in their service and provide for their daily needs.

Since 1872 a monthly missionary magazine has been produced as a focus for news and prayer, and this still remains a central part of Echoes' ministry. Over 6000 missionaries, who have served in nearly 100 countries, have been associated with Echoes of Service, and this represents the largest single Protestant missionary body that has gone out from the U.K. The role of Echoes has grown over the years into that of a service group, which receives and transmits monies, provides care and backup for missionaries and seeks to promote world mission. The missionaries are generally from Christian Brethren churches, those from the U.K. currently numbering about 380, and are serving in over 45 countries. Similar organisations have developed in other countries; some of these are long standing such as Christian Missions in Many Lands (USA), Missionary Service Committee (Canada), Australian Missionary Tidings (Australia), Missionary Services (New Zealand) and Inter-link (Scotland). Newer agencies have emerged in recent years in many countries including Italy, Korea and Malaysia and these represent a truly global outreach.

Ken Fleming during his years in South Africa was linked to Christian Missions in Many Lands, based at New Jersey in the USA, as were his brother Peter Fleming, Ed McCully and Jim Elliot, three of the five martyred in Ecuador in

1956. Their names were also listed on the Echoes Daily Prayer Guide for some years.

For further information contact Echoes office at 1 Widcombe Crescent, Bath, BA2 6AQ or e-mail us at Echoes_of_Service@compuserve.com

Dr Ian Burness
Echoes of Service, Bath